SMALL TALK

by Donna Lynn Thomas

DEDICATION

I'd like to dedicate this book to my husband, whose smiling Irish eyes, easygoing nature, and passion for cooking are every quilter's dream. And, to my sons, Joseph and Peter, who in all their innocence were truly surprised to learn that not all moms quilt. They understood when I was busy and even told their friends on occasion, "Shhh! My mom's working." I love you all more dearly than I can say.

ACKNOWLEDGMENTS

I'd like to pay very special thanks to some wonderful friends:

To Dee Glenn, Sandy Henderson, and Debbie Rose for their absolutely tireless work on pattern testing despite family pressures and assorted flus;

To Gail Drelling for her help;

To Don and Donna Hammond for their patience and computer expertise. They rescued me from many a "desperate" situation;

To Susan Stamilio for quilting, teaching me how to color, and lending a hand with many of the sample illustrations;

To Charlene Joel for editorial suggestions, gentle support, and friendship that only a neighbor "on call" can provide;

To my international friends Ann Marie Eberlin, Marie Therese Ruthsling, Regine Sauder, Martine Ulbig, and Gertrude Hartwig for their quilting services and warm camaraderie;

To Nancy J. Martin and the staff of That Patchwork Place for making it so much easier than I expected.

You've all proved that no quilter stands alone. Thank you from the bottom of my heart.

CREDITS

Photography . . . . Brent Kane
Illustration and Graphics . . . . Stephanie Benson
Text and Cover Design . . . . Judy Petry
Editor . . . . Liz McGehee

That Patchwork Place, Inc., PO Box 118, Bothell, WA 98041-0118

Printed in the Republic of Korea
97 96 95 94 93 92 91 6 5 4 3 2

Library of Congress Cataloging-in-Publication Data

Thomas, Donna Lynn.
Small talk / Donna Lynn Thomas.
p. cm.
ISBN 0-943574-74-9:
1. Machine quilting—Patterns. 2. Patchwork—Patterns. 3. Miniature quilts. I. Title.
TT835.T46 1991 90-48053
746.9'7—dc20 CIP

Susan H. Rountree

Contents

Introduction

"Good things come in small packages." I am not sure what that phrase meant to its creator, but its meaning is clear to a host of quiltmakers who have been seized by the passion to make ever-smaller quilts. This obsession for all things small doesn't stop with quilts. Miniature shops beckon invitingly as does anything tiny, perfect, and intricate. Quiltmakers, however, divert their creative energies into making small quilts. The challenge of making a tiny quilt that is not only mechanically successful but also aesthetically pleasing can be quite exhilarating.

This book is designed to help you translate your quick machine-piecing skills into beautiful miniature works of art. The same techniques used to quickly make large quilts by machine are the best techniques available for making highly accurate miniatures. All the tips included here to help refine your piecing skills for miniatures can be used to improve the quality of your full-size quilts. Accuracy is the most important skill to master, and many tips are provided to achieve that goal. After you are comfortable with the miniature size, you will find that you can put a small quilt together in a few evenings or even a day. You will also acquire skills to help your big quilts just fall together without fudging or making them fit.

When I set out to write this book, I intended to follow a traditional format that put all the skills into one section and the patterns into another. As I was preparing the patterns for testing, I realized that the pattern testers would be shifting back and forth through the skills section of the manuscript trying to find the appropriate technique for a particular pattern.

I decided a different approach might be better. Generally, in a class, students master one set of skills before advancing onto new techniques. Therefore, I have grouped the patterns together with the necessary skills to make them. The book begins by explaining the General Concepts in making miniature quilts, describes the Materials and Equipment necessary to make them, and presents an overview of Basic Skills that pertain to construction of all the quilts in the book. A Gallery of Quilts containing fourteen quilts that I've made begins on page 24 and is provided for your inspiration. The next part is then divided into three sections, each dealing with a different set of skills, and beginning with the simplest in Section I. Each section contains the patterns and techniques appropriate to its level while building onto the skills learned in the previous section. Specific skills followed by a special warm-up project in an intermediate size gradually take the reader from full-size blocks down to the miniature scale. With this method, a reader is not thrown headfirst into the miniature world but first becomes comfortable with the skills mastered on the intermediate-size project.

I hope this approach makes the transition to miniatures even more exciting. I encourage you to take your time and have fun. Above all, be patient with yourself. Others may think you're crazy, but someday they will be in awe of your miniature masterpieces.

Ninepatch *by Donna Lynn Thomas, 1987, Brookhaven, Pennsylvania, 9⅜" x 9⅜". The two-fabric color scheme creates an obvious overall design from this traditional block.*

General Concepts

Miniature quilt blocks have been defined by many as being anywhere from 3" to 6" in size when finished. The blocks in this book are considerably smaller, ranging from 3/4" to about 2" in size with the majority falling in the 1" to 1 1/2" range. It would be difficult to make quilts this size using traditional templates and hand piecing. Fortunately, there is another way to make them.

All the wonderful new methods developed in the last several years using rotary equipment, rulers, sewing machines, and speed techniques are ideal for the accurate construction of tiny quilts. By using the various methods presented in *Small Talk*, you can considerably reduce or, in some cases, eliminate altogether the handling of tiny individual units. At the same time, the accuracy of your piecing will improve. Once you become adept at using these techniques, the joy of working with miniatures will be yours.

SEAM ALLOWANCE

Tiny quilt blocks require tiny seam allowances that are only 1/8" in size. I have tried sewing with a 1/8" seam and found it very frustrating. Many of my students also have found it impossible on their particular sewing machines. Sewing with a standard 1/4" seam allowance that is then cut back to 1/8" is much easier. Technically, this is a waste of fabric but well worth the price in reduced frustration. Be sure you are sewing an accurate 1/4" seam allowance with your machine. Due to the differences between pieces cut from templates and those cut with a rotary cutter, the 1/4" guide on your sewing machine must be checked for accuracy. See page 18 in the Basic Skills section for more information.

ACCURACY

Another important skill to master is a high degree of accuracy in every step of the construction process. I cannot stress enough to take your time, be careful, and think before you cut or sew. The quilt blocks in this book are tiny and were drafted with 1/4" to 3/8" finished-size subunits.

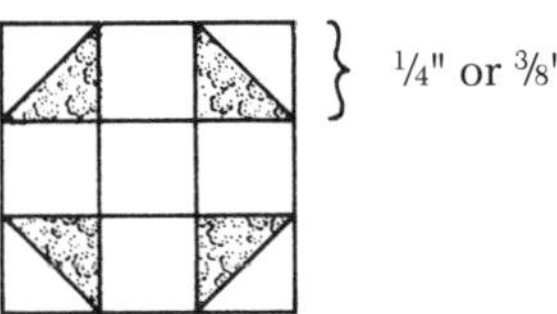

Each block is drafted with either 1/4" or 3/8" subunits. For instance, if the subunit in this Shoo-Fly were 1/4", the block would be 3/4". If the subunits were 3/8", the block would be 1 1/8".

Due to differences in block size, flaws that would appear small on a large quilt block become glaring errors on miniature quilts. For instance, on a Ninepatch block such as Shoo-Fly with its 3/8" patches, an error of 1/32" on one of the subunits translates into the equivalent of a 1" error on a 12" version of the same block. This is not meant to frighten you, but simply to make you aware of the importance of being accurate. You'll be surprised at how accurate you can be with a little practice. If you look closely at the photos of some of the quilts in this book, you will see flaws. As much as we wish it, we can never be perfect—but it sure can be a lot of fun trying!

PATIENCE

Probably the most important concept to master, and perhaps the most difficult, is being patient with yourself. Please keep in mind that making miniatures is something new and different. Think back to the very first quilt you made with all its flaws and how your skills improved with time and practice. The same thing will happen with miniatures: your skills will improve with each tiny quilt you make. Be patient with yourself and have fun—these little ones can be most addictive.

Photo Note

A ruler was included in our quilt photographs to give a size relationship to these charming miniature quilts. The directions and captions give the finished size of each quilt top before layering and quilting. You will notice that the quilts measure slightly smaller in the photos due to shrinkage during quilting and washing.

Materials and Preparation

FABRIC CHOICES

Choosing fabrics for a quilt strikes terror in the heart of many a quilter. Much technical information has been written on the subject by those more knowledgeable than myself, and since I have no formal training in color theory, I will only offer my general approach to making fabric choices, followed by the technical guidelines I find most helpful.

Build a Collection and Practice

It's very important to have a collection of fabrics on hand at home to "play" with. There is not enough time at a shop to lay combinations on the tables and walk away for a few hours before taking a fresh look at what you have put together. Most good shops are very accommodating, but there are limits and other customers. Shop owners would quite justifiably take a dim view of people coming in just to practice combining fabrics, and practice is what it takes to feel comfortable making choices. Therefore, you need to build a collection at home on which to practice.

My favorite therapy on a bad day is to go into my sewing room, select a piece of fabric that I adore, and start pulling others to go with it. It calms and soothes me. I also discover some possibilities that I may not have found in a rush. Since my passion is for multifabric quilts, I do not buy large yardages of most fabrics, especially when I buy for miniatures. Haunt the remnant tables and buy pieces you like as you see them. Trade with friends. Once your collection gets going, you'll be able to put together wonderful personalized combinations that don't look like they came off a manufacturer's coordinated swatch card. There's nothing more depressing than going to a show and seeing several quilts with the same line of fabrics that the original designer used. It's the same as going to a formal dance and seeing five women wearing the same dress.

Play with your collection and you may find that one of those five-year-old fabrics you've been saving is terrific with a three-year-old fabric and that brand new piece you just bought. Practice combining your fabrics even when you are not planning a quilt—it's a good exercise. Be sure to leave your combinations out for a few days, periodically wandering back to view them with a "clean" eye. You'll find yourself making improvements each time until it's just right. Some of my favorite quilts happened as a result of fabric combinations I just had to see as a quilt. In other words, the fabric forced the quilt, not the other way around.

Start with One Print

If you find you have trouble getting started, follow my therapy approach and pull out one multicolored print as your baseline fabric. Start pulling others you feel might go with it and work from there. For instance, take a look at the photo of the Album Quilt on page 24. The baseline fabric for that quilt was the border print, and the other fabrics were pulled to work with it. The only way to feel comfortable making choices is to practice at your leisure—there's no other substitute.

Scale

While playing with your fabrics, keep in mind a few tips to help you make wiser fabric choices. In any quilt, you want to vary the scale, contrast, and color of the prints, but with miniatures, it is equally important to choose fabrics appropriate to the quilt's small size. For instance, that beautiful, large, widely spaced, floral chintz you have in mind for a large quilt will simply not work on a small quilt. Most likely, each piece cut from the floral will look like a completely different fabric due to the wide spacing of the print. If this is the effect you are trying to achieve, then, by all means, go ahead and use it. To see how a particular print will look cut into tiny pieces, make a window template the size of the prospective piece and run it over the fabric. As a general rule, though, it is safer to choose fabrics on a scale appropriate to miniatures and work for variations within this range.

Variety of Print

Use a variety of small prints, such as florals, plaids, checks, dots, and repetitive prints, to keep the quilt visually interesting and to help distinguish one tiny triangle or shape from its neighbor. If you construct a quilt with all similar-type prints, the eye tends to wash and blend the fabrics together, creating a sense of blandness. You would probably never consider using only all checks or pindots in a quilt, so don't make the same mistake with other types of prints. Variety is the key to excitement. You should be able to find a varied selection of medium to small prints that are perfect for miniature quilts. Collect them as you find them so that you can create a working palette of fabrics to draw from when you need to. One-half yard pieces go a long way on quilts this size.

A selection of appropriate fabrics for miniature quilts. Note the variety of print, scale, color, and contrast.

Contrast

Another important way to create visual interest and help distinguish shapes is to maintain high contrast among your fabrics. Contrast refers to the lightness and darkness of fabrics in relation to each other. Two dark fabrics have low contrast in relation to each other just as two light fabrics do. In most cases, the contrast between fabrics in a miniature needs to be higher. Take a look at the photograph of the Cake Stand quilt below. The contrast between the pink triangles and the background print is not high enough, and as a result, the triangle points tend to wash into the background. The green print is overpowering, further diminishing the visibility of the Cake Stand blocks. As you can see, care is especially important as you choose the fabrics for small quilts.

On the other hand, avoid using fabrics that have a print involving a lot of contrast within itself. An example of this would be a deep red print with lots of white swirling flowers all over it. When such a fabric is put next to a light print or muslin, it will look like chunks are missing where the white in the print meets the muslin or light fabric. The sides of the tiny triangles and squares in a miniature are not long enough for your eye to fill in the blanks to create a continuous line. Stick to subtly printed fabrics to avoid this pitfall.

Another poor fabric combination occurs when a multicolored print lies next to a fabric similar in color to one of the colors in the multiprint. Look at the photo of the Ohio Star quilt below. Notice how some of the star points, where the rosebuds on the black print meet the pink fabric, bleed into each other. Try to anticipate situations such as this when choosing your fabrics.

***Cake Stand** by Donna Lynn Thomas, 1989, Frankfurt, West Germany, 9⅞" x 12". Notice the poor choice of fabrics in the pieced blocks. Because there is not enough contrast between the fabrics, the triangle points blend into the background fabric. The green print also overpowers the rest of the quilt, leaving it out of balance.*

***Ohio Star** by Donna Lynn Thomas, 1989, Frankfurt, West Germany, 7⅜" x 7⅜". The pink rosebuds in the black print lie next to the pink triangles, causing the Ohio Star points to bleed into each other.*

Variety of Color

Color is another useful tool for creating interesting miniature quilts. Color families can be used in place of contrast to help distinguish one part of the quilt from another. For instance, if you have a situation that calls for two fabrics of relatively equal contrast, try to use prints in two different color families, such as red and green, to help delineate the shapes. Color can also be used to strengthen or soften the contrast between two fabrics. A dark blue next to a pale rose will produce a bolder, more delineated shape than a dark blue next to a pale blue. A monochromatic color scheme will be softer than a quilt of many colors but requires more careful handling of contrast among the fabrics. What you choose all depends on what you are trying to achieve.

Snow Patch *by Donna Lynn Thomas, 1990, Frankfurt, West Germany, 10¾" x 10¾". Color rather than contrast is used here to delineate the squares in the Ninepatch blocks. Quilted by Marie-Therese Rutsling.*

Creating Scrap Quilts

Multifabric quilts are regaining popularity, but many quilters are not sure how to choose fabrics for a scrap quilt. Here are two methods to help make the process less intimidating.

Looking at the quilt block(s) you wish to make, assign grades of contrast to each position in the pattern. It can be helpful to draw the block out in line form and color it in with blacks, whites, and shades of gray. Sort your fabrics into piles of darks, mediums, and lights, regardless of color. You can define your piles more precisely if you like with such labels as very dark, dark, medium dark, medium, etc. Once the fabrics are sorted, the piles can be assigned to positions in the block diagram, and you are ready to begin cutting. When you work with miniatures, it is extremely important to keep the contrast between shapes high, or the boundaries between them will blur, especially with multifabric quilts.

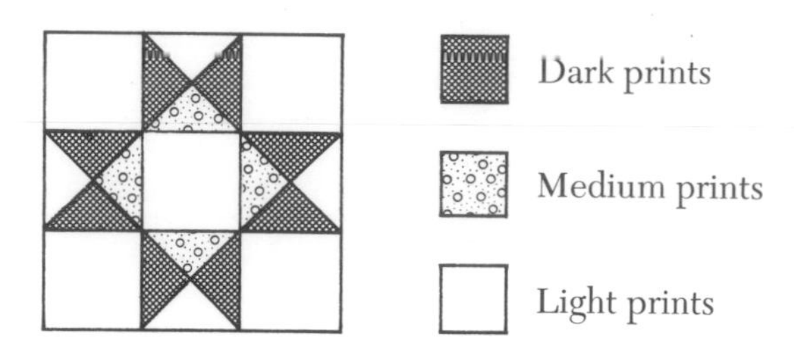

In a manner similar to contrast, different color families can be assigned to various positions in a block design. The color families can also be divided into contrast groups, such as dark blue, medium blue, etc. Nancy J. Martin and Marsha McCloskey call this a color recipe. This color recipe system is perfect for working with miniature scrap quilts because the use of both color and high contrast will better define the small shapes. There are many examples of scrap quilts in this book. See if you can identify which of the two methods was used to create each quilt.

Fabric Content

I strongly suggest the use of only 100% quilt-weight cotton fabrics for miniatures. They are not slippery, tend to stay where you put them, and crease well. Look for fine, tightly woven, high-quality cottons. Gauzy fabrics will not hold together in a miniature, and heavy cottons will be too thick to look like they belong. Avoid synthetic fibers, as they tend to fray more readily—a highly undesirable trait when your finished seam is only ⅛".

Try to resist the temptation to buy heavily discounted fabrics. Generally, they are made from inferior cotton goods and printed with inferior dyes. Just as in meats and other commodities, there are various grades of basic cotton goods. You are not going to get premium grades at bargain basement prices. I encourage you to buy your quilt fabrics at reputable quilt shops, as they buy top-grade fabrics specifically for quilters. As the saying goes, "You get what you pay for." Buy the best to make the best or you will find yourself disappointed in the end.

Keeping all these tidbits in mind, sort through your fabric collection, scraps and all, and separate the fabrics suitable for miniatures. You'll need a good selection of dark, medium, and light prints with a small to medium scale and in a variety of colors. Take note of what you have and keep an eye out at your local quilt shops for what you may need to fill in the gaps. Remember to look for variety of print, scale, color, and contrast in your selections. If you're buying or trading with friends, look for quarter-yard pieces, fat quarters (half-yard pieces cut in half on the fold, approximately 18" x 22"), or even half-yards. An odd-size square is more useful than a long, skinny piece, although I wouldn't discard that skinny piece either—you never know where you might be able to use it! Start playing with your fabrics, come up with some combinations that are pleasing to your eye, and you'll feel your confidence grow.

FABRIC PRETREATMENT

The first thing you should do with a fabric that will be used in one of your quilts is to test it for bleeding. A few years ago, I attended an extremely informative lecture and workshop given by Harriet Hargrave, a well-known quilter, author, and textile expert. Her instructions for pretesting and treating fabrics made a great deal of sense, and I have been using them successfully ever since.

The Bleeding Test

To test fabrics for bleeding, fill a pint-size jar with boiling water and add a 2"–3" scrap of fabric for about twenty minutes. Each fabric should be tested individually in fresh water. After twenty minutes, check the water for signs of color. If it's still clear, the fabric is safe to use. If not, the fabric may be releasing excess dye and should be further tested to determine if the dye will transfer to other fabrics. Place the wet scrap in a fresh jar of boiling water with a piece of unbleached muslin for twenty minutes to test for transfer of dyes, such as could occur during the wet washing of a whole quilt. Once this test is passed, place the two wet scraps on top of each other on a plate to test for surface transfer of dyes, such as could occur while a completed quilt is drying. Again, wait twenty minutes. If no dye transfer occurs, the fabric is safe to use. If the fabric fails either of the last two tests, do not use it in your quilt. Vinegar and salt baths are only temporary measures that do not last. Eventually, the fabric will bleed again. If you're using fabrics from your scrap bag, they should already have passed the bleeding test when you originally used the fabric. If you're not sure, test them again.

Prewashing

Whether or not to prewash your fabrics depends on your preferences. I don't feel strongly one way or the other, but there are several points to consider when making your decision. The first point concerns the matter of preshrinking the fabrics for a quilt. Industry experts say the standards for premium-quality cotton goods are fairly consistent and, therefore, the fabrics should shrink equally. Also, if you are using a cotton batt that will not be preshrunk, it may be a good idea not to preshrink your fabric so that the fabric and batt shrink together. By the same token, it might be wise to preshrink cotton fabrics when a polyester batt is going to be used.

Another point to consider is that fabric is generally dusty and sometimes lightly soiled by the time you buy it at the shop. It's nice to start with clean materials. Also, if you are looking for a more malleable fabric for handwork, prewashing will remove the sizing added to fabric that gives it more body and a slightly stiffer hand. If your needs call for the extra body the sizing provides, avoid prewashing. I find the extra body helpful when working with the smaller pieces of a miniature quilt, so I tend not to prewash. Of course, if one fabric going into a quilt is already prewashed, then all fabrics should be washed to avoid uneven shrinking. A light application of spray sizing can be added to replace the original sizing.

Soaps and Detergents

If, after the bleeding tests, you choose to prewash your fabric, do not use detergents, as they can destroy the bond between a color dye and cotton fibers. Once this bond is destroyed, a fabric tends to bleed with the passage of time. A capful of plain, sudsy ammonia in a sinkful of water is a good, inexpensive cleanser (use ¼ cup for a washer load). Some other soaps that are available are grated Fels Naptha® soap, Orvus® horse paste (traditionally located at feed and tack shops but now found at some quilt shops as quilt soap), and old-fashioned lye soap. Use ¼ cup of any of these cleansers in a washer load or about a tablespoonful for the sink. Ensure Quilt Wash™ is also safe for fabric prewashing. Follow the package instructions for its use.

Water Temperature

Other than scraps of fabric for the bleeding test, fabric should never be exposed to very hot or very cold water. Since extreme water temperatures are damaging to natural fibers, use only a water temperature that is suitable for a baby when washing both fabric and completed quilts. Once washed, let the fabric air dry, or machine fluff on low temperature until just damp, and press it smooth.

BATTINGS AND THREADS

Battings

In the past, I have used an assortment of different types of batts, trying to achieve an appropriate look for miniature quilts. Regular-size batts, even light batts, made the quilts too thick and stiff to drape like a large quilt does. The finished quilts tended to look like potholders. Flannel was too heavy and had too little loft. Finally, after much searching, I discovered that the perfect batt for miniatures is a 100% cotton batt peeled in half. The newer 100% cotton batts peel nicely and are exactly the loft needed for a miniature quilt.

The other wonderful quality of a cotton batt is that it shrinks, giving the miniatures a "real" quilt look with that soft, old patina so reminiscent of antique quilts. This antique-quilted look is greatly enhanced when fabrics are not prewashed and thus shrink along with the cotton batt. Take note of this as you look at the photos of the quilts in this book.

A peeled cotton batt also enables you to reduce the size of your quilting stitches to a scale compatible with a miniature quilt. On the other hand, more stitching is required for a peeled cotton batt, along with extra care in laundering (see Care of Miniatures on page 86).

Threads

Ideally, the threads in a quilt should never be stronger than the fibers in the fabric. In other words, the fiber content should match between thread and fabric. As time passes, polyester threads can cut cotton and should not be used. Threads of 100% cotton are best but, if unavailable, the second best choice is a cotton-covered polyester thread. Never skimp on the quality of your thread or fabrics, since the quality and integrity of your quilt are only as high as the quality of the materials that go into it.

Rather than constantly changing the spool and bobbin thread color to match the darkest fabric in a seam, I keep a variety of shades of gray on hand. Wind three bobbins, one with dark gray, one with medium gray, and one with light gray threads, and use the one closest to the value of the darkest fabric. For instance, a dark gray thread should be used with dark fabrics and a light gray with light fabrics. If neutral or cream-based fabrics are being sewn, use a neutral or cream-colored thread. Keep in mind that your thread should never be darker than your darkest dark or lighter than your lightest light. As a rule, you should have no trouble with threads showing at a seam if the thread is close to the value of the darkest fabric in the seam.

Equipment

ROTARY EQUIPMENT AND RULERS

Rotary equipment is essential to the accurate construction of miniature quilts since, when properly used, it enhances the accuracy of your cutting. It is important to use the best equipment that you can afford. There are many brands on the market, and innovations and improvements are constantly being made. Keep in touch with your local quilt shops concerning new equipment and its reliability, as most shops introduce and try new items as they are presented to the industry.

Rotary Cutters

A rotary cutter is a round-bladed cutting instrument attached to a handle. It looks like a pizza cutter with a protective shield that is either manually or automatically released, depending on the model. Rotary cutters come in two different sizes—large and small. For miniatures, I prefer the small rotary cutter because it is easier to handle in small areas. Be sure to keep several replacement blades on hand. You will need them when the cutter accidentally rolls over a pin or lands on a concrete floor, and the shops are closed for the night.

Rotary Mat

You must have a rotary mat to use with your rotary cutter. If you try to cut fabric with your cutter on anything but a mat specifically made for rotary cutters, you will immediately ruin both your blade and the cutting surface.

An 18" x 24" rotary mat is a nice size mat to have if you are purchasing one for the first time. It is large enough to accommodate the folded width of a piece of fabric but small enough to be toted to workshops. Always store your mat flat and keep it away from extreme temperatures that can warp it irreparably.

Quilter's Rulers

In addition to a rotary cutter and mat, a good quilter's ruler is an invaluable tool. There are many types of rulers now available, ranging from highly specialized tools to general purpose rulers. If you are like many quilters, you probably already own a number of rulers. Look for the following desirable features to determine if you already have what you need:

Since the quilts in *Small Talk* deal with very small subunits, a ruler with 1/8" markings is absolutely necessary. You do not want to guess where the 1/8" mark would be on a ruler with 1/4" grid lines. These 1/8" marks should appear on every inch line both horizontally and vertically.

Rulers that are 24" long are generally too big and clumsy for miniature work, so choose one that is 12"–18" in length. For rotary cutting, it is also important to use a hard plastic ruler that is at least 1/8" thick, as soft plastic rulers are easily cut by the sharp rotary blade. A "window" at each inch line intersection is also helpful in guaranteeing that the edge of your fabric is where it ought to be in relation to the markings. Generally, a 3" wide ruler is sufficient for miniature work, but a 6" wide ruler will also work.

It is helpful to have a small 1" x 6" or 1" x 12" ruler near the sewing machine for checking seams and even to do some of the finer cutting. Again, this small ruler is useless unless it also has 1/8" marks on all four sides and throughout the middle. See Basic Skills, page 11, for instructions on how to use rotary equipment and rulers.

The Bias Square®

The Bias Square® is one specialty ruler that should be in every quick-piecing quilter's inventory. It enables you to construct presewn bias squares with an ease not previously possible.

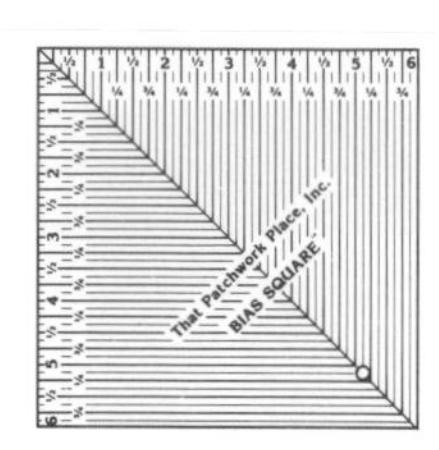

The Bias Square®

A bias square is a square composed of two right triangles sewn together on their long edges. To better understand the concept, draw a square with a line cutting it in half on the diagonal. Normally, but not always, the straight of grain runs along the outside edges.

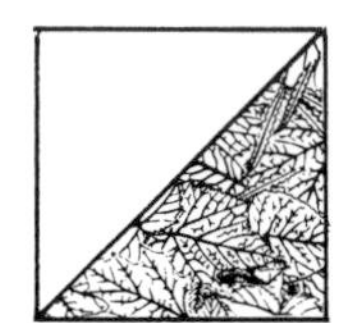

Straight of grain (S-O-G)

Until the Bias Square was introduced several years ago, the most advanced way to preassemble bias squares was to draw grid lines on two layers of fabric, sew the layers together on the lines, and then cut the grids apart. Unfortunately, this method had too many variables that increased the chances of inaccuracy with each step. The new bias-square method and the Bias Square were exactly what was needed to enable quilters to construct highly accurate, tiny bias squares without frustration. Since the degree of accuracy is considerably greater and more easily attained with this new method, I have used it to construct all bias squares in this book. See Section II: Bias Squares, pages 45–48, for directions on how to construct bias squares with the Bias Square.

SEWING MACHINE

Many types of sewing machines are available. Some are more expensive than others and some make the job easier, but as long as they can sew a good straight stitch, most can be used successfully to make miniature quilts.

Your machine should be cleaned after each use and oiled routinely according to your service manual's instructions. I have to admit that I am guilty of neglect on occasion, but I do clean and oil my machine frequently. Daily maintenance involves opening the bobbin housing and cleaning the area with a brush to remove lint and loose dirt. It is not wise to blow into the machine, as the moisture in your breath can cause the interior of the machine to rust.

Machine Needles

The size of the machine needle you use varies, depending on the fabric you are working with. For cottons, and miniatures in particular, I suggest the use of very fine machine needles to reduce the drag on the small pieces of fabric that are being sewn. If the needle is fine, it is less likely to "eat" your fabric (pull the fabric pieces under the throat plate). For the same reason, it is a good idea to change your needle frequently, as it will become dull with use.

Straight-Stitch Throat Plate

Another piece of equipment that is helpful in keeping the fabric from being eaten is a straight-stitch throat plate. Most machines come equipped with a throat plate that has an oval opening to accommodate the side-to-side movement of a needle as it performs a zigzag stitch. A straight-stitch throat plate has a small round opening that can only be used when the needle is in the center position and sewing a straight stitch. It is not available for all machines, nor is it necessary for all machines, but it can help solve this particular problem.

ADDITIONAL SEWING SUPPLIES

Besides the basic equipment already discussed, you will need to have on hand a few important supplies. Items such as thread clips, odds and ends of template plastic, quilting needles, thread, fabric shears, and pins are probably already present in your inventory and don't need further discussion. In addition, a small bit of embroidery floss will be required for certain patterns. Washable markers are handy for marking appliqué pieces.

Another item that you most likely have, an ordinary seam ripper, will be used in a way you may not have thought of before. If you don't have one, I urge you to acquire one. Its special use as a "better finger" will be discussed in the Basic Skills section, page 19, and may prove to be invaluable. Last but not least, keep a clean iron and spray-mist bottle handy near the work area for pressing your little treasures as they are created.

Basic Skills

ROTARY CUTTING

All the instructions in this book are based on rotary cutting and, therefore, pattern templates are not given. Due to the size of the pieces in miniature quilts, modern rotary and machine-piecing techniques are eminently more desirable than hand piecing or template-marked machine piecing. All cutting dimensions include ¼" seam allowances, as do all measurements found in diagrams and discussion, unless specifically designated as finished size. DO NOT ADD SEAM ALLOWANCES.

Grain Line

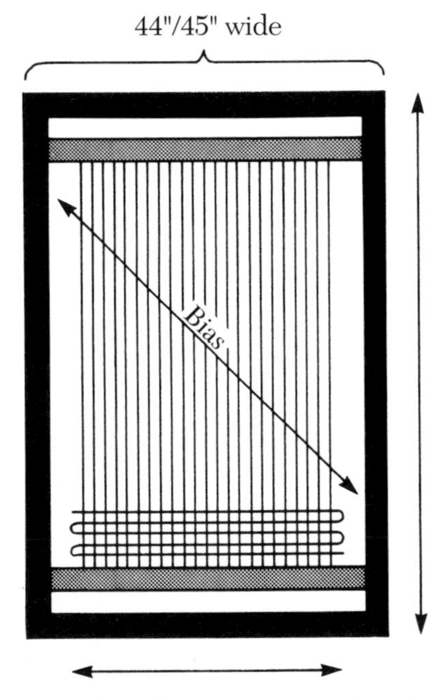

Warp threads form the lengthwise grain. The warp threads on either side form the fabric selvages after the weft threads are woven in.

Weft threads are woven back and forth through the warp threads to form the crosswise grain

It is helpful to understand the weaving process in order to understand why each type of grain has its own special properties. When fabric is woven on a hand loom, the process begins with the long warp threads attached to the front bar of the loom. If ten yards of fabric are desired, then the warp threads are cut ten yards long, and the ends are rolled tightly on a bar on the opposite side of the loom. There are as many threads lined up across the front bar as are needed to make the fabric as wide as desired. When the fabric is finished, these warp threads are referred to as the lengthwise grain of the fabric.

Once the warp threads are secured in place on the loom, threads are wound on a shuttle and woven back and forth from side to side through the warp threads. These new side-to-side weft threads are referred to as the crosswise grain of the finished fabric. The process, though simplified, is the same process used in modern, mechanized fabric production.

Lengthwise grain has little to no give. This is the result of the warp threads being tightly secured at both ends during the weaving process. The lack of give means that edges cut parallel to this grain will not stretch with handling.

Crosswise grain has a slight amount of give, since the weft threads are not secured to anything except the warp threads when woven from side to side. Even so, the thread itself will only give so far, depending on the quality of the thread used. Edges cut parallel to the crosswise grain can stretch slightly if roughly handled. Cutting on either the lengthwise or crosswise grain is considered to be cutting on grain, unless a pattern specifically instructs you to cut on one type of grain instead of the other.

Bias is anything other than lengthwise or crosswise grain, although true bias is defined as the direction running at a 45° angle to the other grains. Think of the lengthwise and crosswise grains as forming a square. Bias runs from corner to corner across the diagonal of the square. It has a generous amount of give when pulled since there are no diagonal threads restraining it. A great deal of care must be exercised when handling edges cut parallel to the bias. They can easily become distorted, stretched, and wavy if pulled and overhandled.

Generally, when making quilts, we try to cut our shapes as close to straight-of-grain (S-O-G) as possible. It's difficult to cut rotary strips that are true S-O-G, so we settle for "close" grain with quite satisfactory results. Due to the quirks of mass production, few fabrics are printed on grain, and many are stretched off grain when rolled onto bolts for sale. A piece of fabric that is badly off grain can be pulled straight by gently holding opposite diagonal corners and pulling until the threads are back in line. Most miniatures can be constructed from scraps, and it's fairly easy to straighten the small pieces and then cut close to true S-O-G strips for your quilts.

All squares, strips, and rectangles should be cut on grain. Triangles, being three-sided, cannot have all their edges cut on grain. Therefore, it is a good idea to look at the position of the triangle in the pattern and consider a few guidelines when deciding which edges should be cut on grain.

1. Place all edges on the perimeter of a quilt block on grain so that the block does not stretch out of shape.
2. Whenever possible, without violating rule 1, sew a bias edge to a straight edge to stabilize the seam.

Neither one of these rules is absolute; there are exceptions to both rules in the patterns found in this book. To help tame bias edges, apply a little spray sizing to the fabric. It's not a miracle cure, but it does help.

Preparing the Fabric Edges for Cutting

Since miniatures do not require large pieces of fabric, you will most likely be working with nothing larger than a fat quarter (a half-yard cut in half on the fold, approximately 18" x 22"). If the piece of fabric is full size (44" wide), please cut it in half, as the additional width will be a hindrance. It's also a good time to remove the selvage. Although it indicates straight-of-grain, the selvage is rarely a straight edge itself.

Place the edge of your quilter's ruler on grain just inside the selvage. Be sure to hold the ruler absolutely still with a firm downward pressure and fingers spread wide so that the ruler does not shift. Some quilters find it helpful to anchor their ruler by placing their outer fingers or the palm of their hand to the left of the ruler, on the rotary mat.

Retract the rotary cutter's safety mechanism, place the blade next to the ruler's edge, and begin to cut slowly away from you. As the blade rolls along the ruler's edge, it may sometimes be necessary to slowly and carefully "walk" your hands up the ruler. Be careful not to shift the ruler out of line. Cut completely past the opposite edge and engage the safety mechanism again before putting the cutter back on the table. Make this a routine safety precaution. This newly cut edge is now your straight-of-grain edge. Reverse these instructions if you are left-handed.

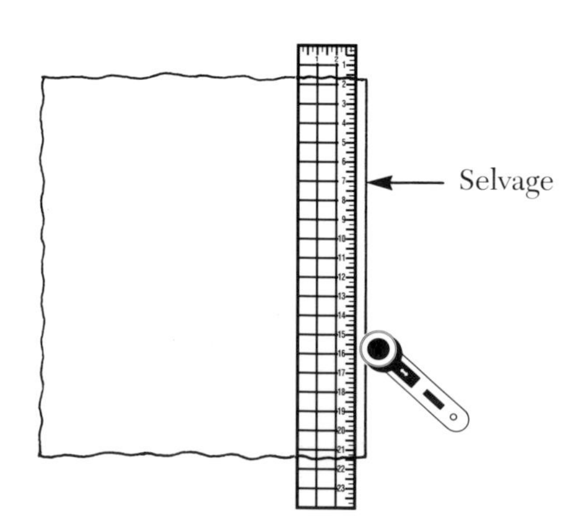

Remove the selvage to create the straight-of-grain edge

Now, make another straight cut at a right angle to the first cut. Arrange the fabric with the straight-of-grain edge on the bottom facing toward you and the bulk of the fabric to the right. In order to create a right-angle guide, lay one edge of the Bias Square® along the bottom edge of the fabric. Put the long edge of your quilter's ruler next to the Bias Square, as shown in the illustration; then, remove the Bias Square and make a cut to the right of your ruler.

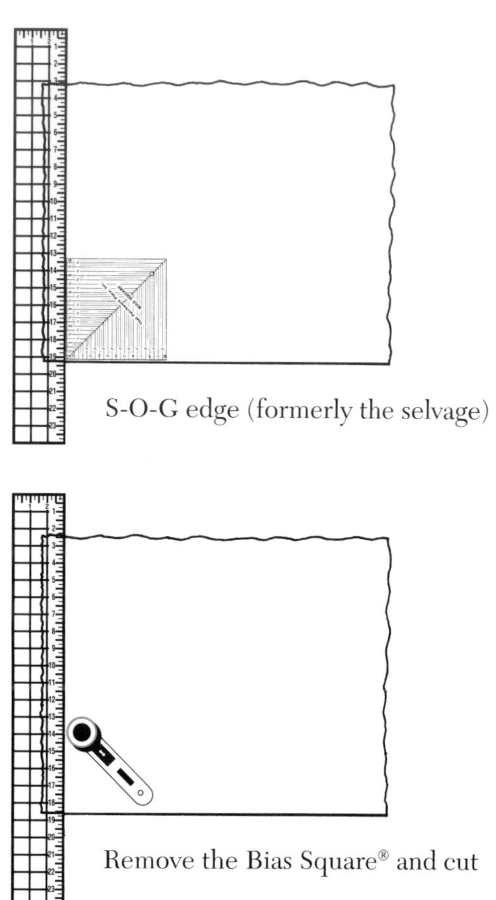

S-O-G edge (formerly the selvage)

Remove the Bias Square® and cut

If your fabric is longer than your ruler, you may fold it in half and use the fold to align the Bias Square. However, you must first place the fold on grain so that the cut edges will be on grain also.

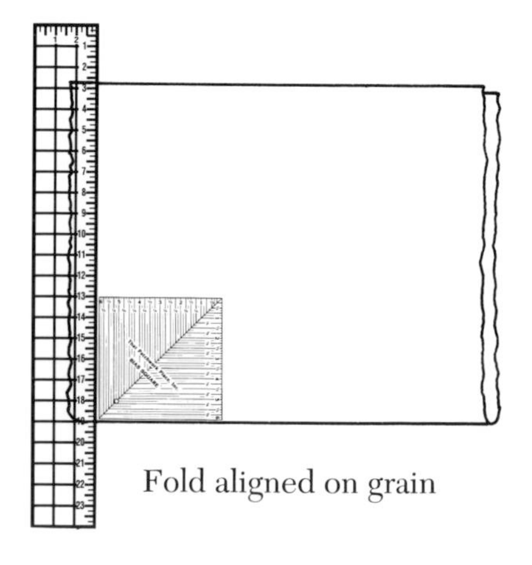

Fold aligned on grain

Cutting Strips

Strips are always cut with the right-angle corner on the lower left. The rest of the fabric lies to the right. Let's say you want to cut a 1" strip that will be 1/2" when finished. Find the 1" line inside the right edge of your ruler and align that marking with the prepared left edge of the fabric. In addition, always have one of the ruler's horizontal lines even with the bottom edge of the fabric. If, after cutting a few strips, you can no longer align both a horizontal and vertical line at the same time, you need to recut the left edge to be at right angles to the bottom. This is particularly important if you are cutting folded fabric. If the cut is not at a right angle to the fold, you will end up with a "bent" strip. Strips are always cut 1/2" wider than the desired finished size to allow for the two side seams.

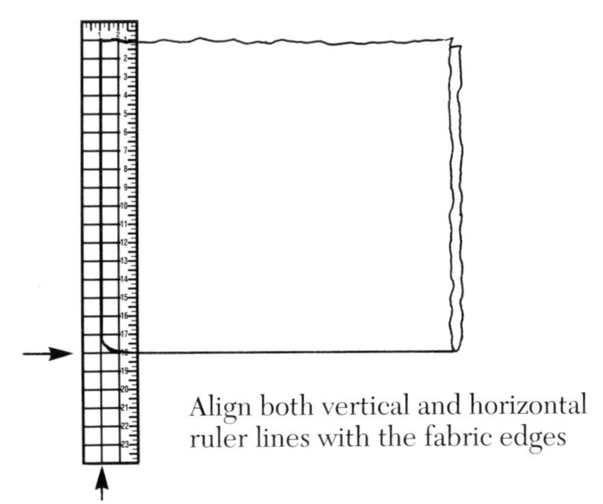

Align both vertical and horizontal ruler lines with the fabric edges

To cut a strip of a particular length, line up the ruler to the proper length from the bottom at the same time as you line up the width lines. A quick slice across the top of the ruler after completing the upward cut will yield a strip of specified length. In such a case, you would not extend your upward cut all the way past the top raw edge of the fabric. Since many of you may be working with limited scraps, it's important to use fabric efficiently.

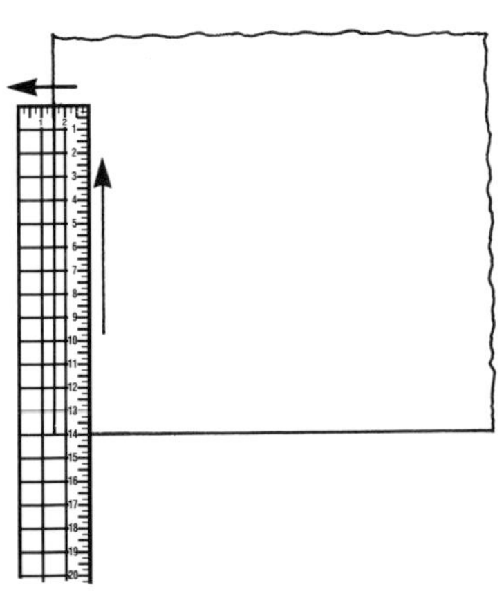

It is also possible to adjust the length of the strips called for in a pattern. Often, the size scrap you have may not be the exact dimension called for in the pattern. Always cut the largest pieces first and then readjust the rest of the cutting. A set of long strips for a particular strata can be replaced with twice as many shorter strips and twice as many strata assembled. Rather than cut exactly one-half the original length, cut the strips for the new strata a little longer, just in case. For example, the 15" long strips required for a 15" strata can be cut into twice as many 8" strips and two sets of assembled 8" strata.

Cutting Squares

Squares are cut easily from strips. If 1 1/2" squares are needed, cut a 1 1/2" strip, turn the short end of the strip facing left and start cutting 1 1/2" squares off the end. Be sure to align a horizontal line across the bottom each time you prepare to cut, just as you do when cutting strips.

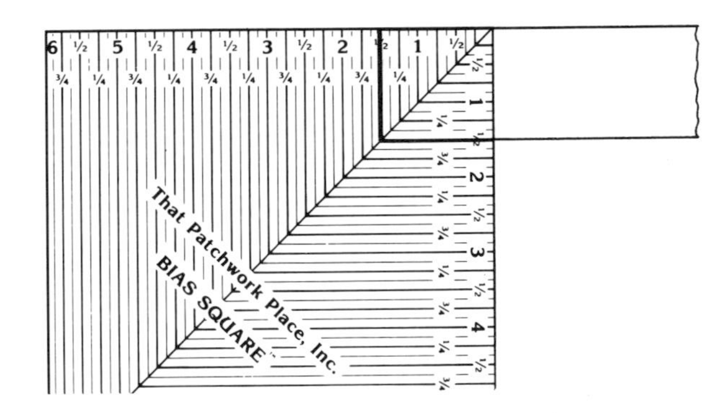

If, for instance, you need only one or two squares, the Bias Square® is an excellent tool to accomplish the task. Lay the Bias Square on the lower left prepared fabric corner, with the appropriate marks on the fabric edges. A neat slice, up and across, yields the square.

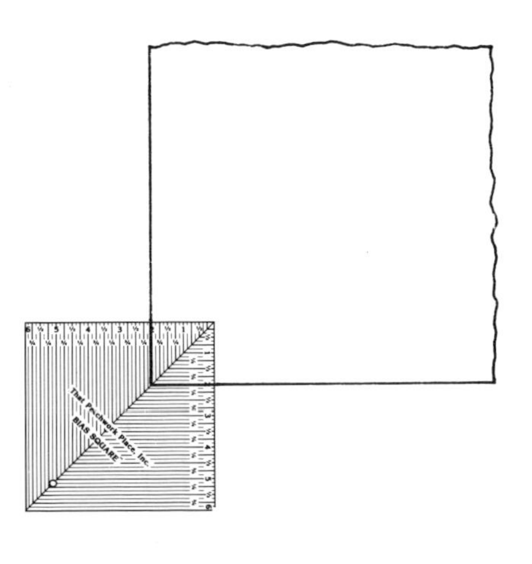

Cutting Triangles

There are two ways to cut triangles. The method you use depends on which edge the straight-of-grain should be placed. Nevertheless, both methods start with a square that is subcut into either two or four triangles.

Half-square triangle: This type of triangle is created by cutting a square in half on the diagonal to yield two triangles. In this case, the straight-of-grain is on the two edges adjacent to the right-angle corner.

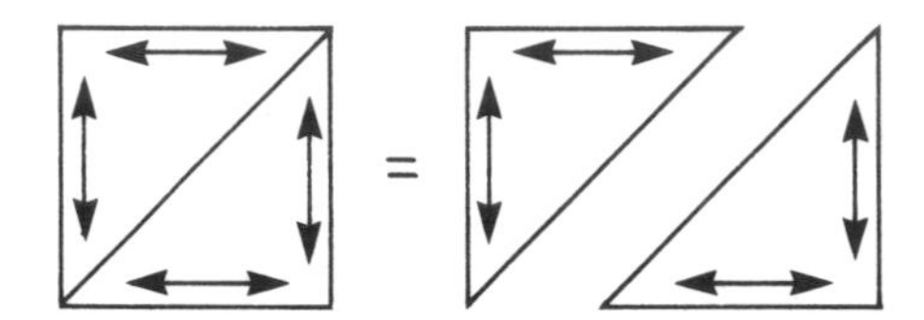

To compute the size square to cut, you must first determine the finished size of the short edge of the triangle. Add ⅞" to this figure and cut a square this size. Then, cut the square in half on the diagonal. Once all seams are sewn on the triangle, it will be the size you originally determined.

For example: To produce two finished-size 1" right triangles, add ⅞" to 1" to equal 1⅞". Cut a square this size and cut it in half on the diagonal.

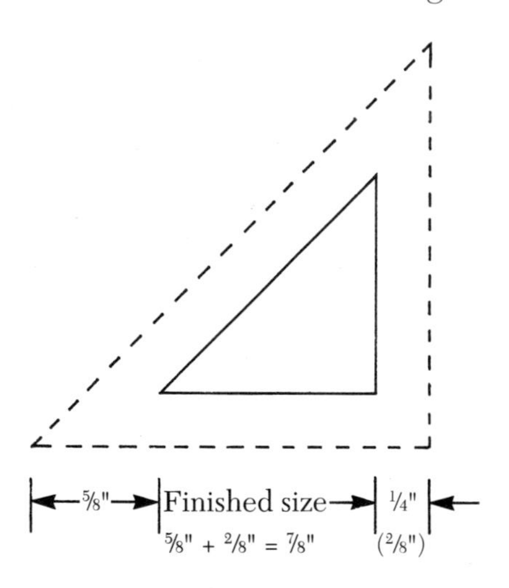

Quarter-square triangle: This type of triangle is created by cutting a square in half on the diagonal in both directions. A triangle cut in this fashion has the straight-of-grain on its long side only.

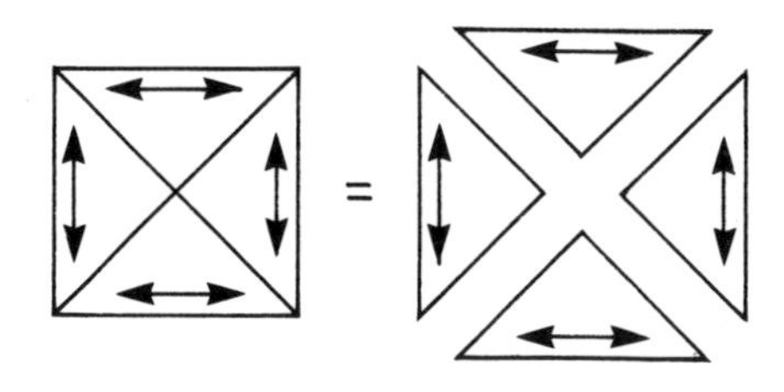

To compute the size square needed for this method, you must determine the finished size of the long side of the triangle. To this figure, add 1¼" and cut a square that size. Now, cut the square in half on both diagonals.

For example: To produce four triangles with a finished size of 1" on the long edges, add 1¼" to 1" to equal 2¼". Cut a square this size and cut it in half on both diagonals.

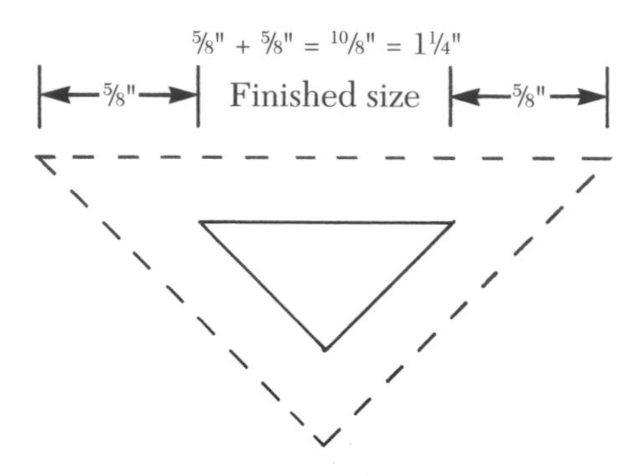

Many times quarter-square triangles are used for the set-in corner triangles of a quilt block. In such a case, it is wise to overestimate the finished size of the triangles and then cut them to size after the quilt top or block is assembled.

Fabric Requirements

Since you will probably be using scraps and odd-size pieces for the patterns in this book, the fabric requirements given are only a guide. To be sure you have enough of a scrap fabric, multiply the two dimensions (length x width) given in the pattern cutting requirements to find the total number of square inches. Then, do the same for the scrap you wish to use for that particular piece. As long as the total square inches of your scrap is the same or preferably larger than the pattern's, you should be able to use the scrap. It's always better to err on the side of excess when dealing with fabric quantities. Remember that you can always cut more strips of smaller size or fewer of longer length to accommodate an odd shape.

SEWING

The sewing machine and rotary equipment complement each other perfectly. Just as with cutting, if care is taken in the sewing process, a high degree of accuracy is easily attainable. Before starting to sew, you must be able to produce a consistently accurate ¼" seam allowance so your pieces will fit together nicely. The following sections will help you do this. Take the time now to use the strip test and adjust your machine as necessary. You'll save yourself an untold amount of frustration in the future.

The Rotary-Cut Seam Allowance

There is a distinct difference between what happens when sewing a hand-marked seam and when sewing an unmarked rotary-cut piece. Fabric pieces that have accurate template-marked seam lines consistently fit together whether sewing by hand or machine. The key, of course, is in the accuracy of the quiltmaker. Many quilters find that their rotary-cut pieces don't always fit as well as hand-marked pieces, no matter how accurate they have been. Just the same, most are unconcerned with the small discrepancies when trying to assemble various patterns and quilt blocks, and simply "make" them fit. The small inconvenience becomes a major problem, though, when one sews miniatures. What was a small error on a full-size quilt becomes a glaring error on a miniature. For instance, a ⅛"–¼" error can be accommodated on a 12" block but is intolerable on a ¾" block. That ⅛" error would translate into a 2" error on the same full-size block! There isn't any way to "make" that fit.

This seam allowance phenomenon has puzzled me for several years and consumed many a sleepless night. After much reflection and thought, the reason seems clear—the loss of a pencil line makes the difference. To find out why this is true, draw a perfect 2" square on a piece of ⅛" graph paper and make an accurate template from this square. Trace around the template onto a smooth piece of muslin, add a ¼" seam allowance, and cut it out. This type of marked square can be sewn to another piece by either hand or machine, simply by aligning and stitching on the pencil lines. Now, using your rotary cutter and ruler, cut a perfect 2½" square (2" plus the two ¼" seams on either side of the square). A rotary-cut square is sewn by aligning the raw edges with the ¼" guide of a sewing machine and stitching without benefit of a pencil line. Lay these two squares in front of you and refer to them as you read further.

Looking at the template-marked square, you will see three identifiable areas on the fabric. First, there is the 2" dimension of the square, which lies just INSIDE the pencil line (when you trace AROUND the template, you are tracing AROUND the 2" square). Next, there is the pencil line itself, which occupies a thin but very real space. Last, there is the ¼" seam allowance, which lies on the OTHER SIDE of the pencil line. When properly sewn, the thread will occupy the same space as the pencil line. As a result, the 2" square lies inside the actual stitching line and the seam allowance lies outside of it.

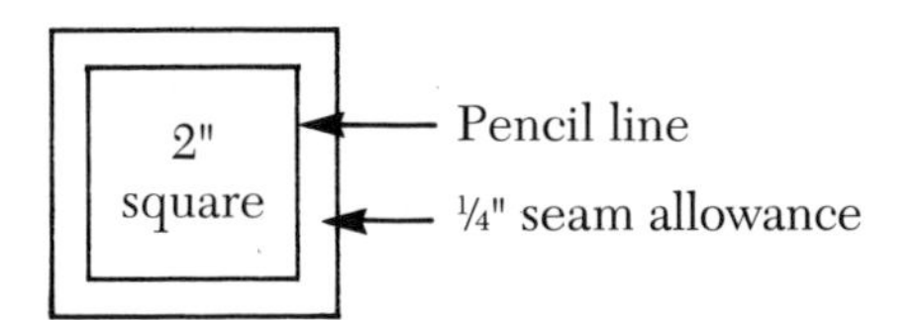

The thread of stitching line will occupy same space as pencil line

Now, take a look at the unmarked rotary-cut square. There are only two areas to this piece. There is the 2" square and right next to it, unseparated by a pencil line's distance, is the ¼" seam allowance. Where is the thin area of the stitching line taken from? If the seam allowance measures a full ¼" from the raw edge up to but not including the stitching line, then the stitching line is occupying space to the left of the seam allowance inside the area of the 2" square. The 2" square is then decreased in size on all four sides an amount equal to the size of the stitching line (about 1/16" for each seam).

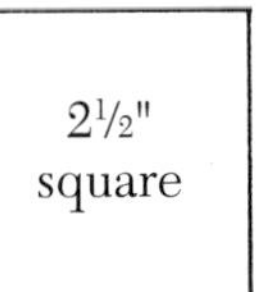

There is no pencil line on a 2½" rotary-cut square

This is what routinely happens when you sew rotary-cut pieces. Granted, a pencil line does not seem like much to worry about, and it isn't a big problem on most large quilts without any other inaccuracies. But, what about a block such as the Schoolhouse where there may be eight seams across the top and four across the bottom? That small discrepancy translates into a ½" loss at the top and a ¼" loss at the bottom, resulting in a not-so-square block. I'll bet a number of you have experienced this problem with other designs, too. How many times have your pieced Irish Chain blocks been smaller than their lightly pieced alternate blocks? Now, translate this potential loss to a miniature quilt and the value of an accurately sewn seam becomes extremely important.

The solution is to make sure the stitching line is taken from the dimension of the seam allowance, not the square. To do this, sew a scant ¼" seam. If this thought confuses you, just think of it as measuring your full ¼" seam to include the stitching line, i.e., from the raw edge of the fabric to the left side of the needle.

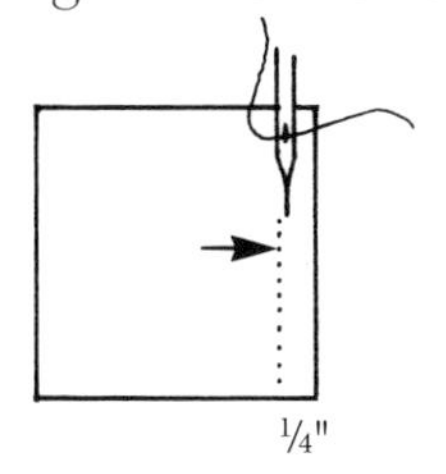

The stitching line must occupy space within the boundaries of the ¼" seam allowance, not the 2" square. Therefore, the seam allowance must measure ¼" from the raw edge of the square to the left side of the needle.

Some machine guides already include the stitching line as part of the seam allowance, whether intentionally or not. That is why it is important to test your own machine to see how it "measures up." The strip test that follows will tell you whether your seam guide is correct.

I've included this explanation to satisfy the curiosity of those of you who, like myself, aren't satisfied doing something new until they know the reason why. For those of you who got lost a few paragraphs back, trust me, test your machines and put the explanation out of your mind for the present time. Maybe in a little while, it will make more sense. No matter what the case, use this new seam guide on all your quilts, both large and small, and discover how they just fall together. It really works!

Testing Your Machine's 1/4" Sewing Guide

Due to the peculiarities of machine piecing without a template-marked sewing guide, it is imperative that you check the accuracy of your sewing machine's 1/4" sewing guide. Most machines use the edge of the standard presser foot as the 1/4" guide unless a mark is provided on the throat plate. The following simple test will help you gauge your machine's accuracy.

Cut three sets of strips that are exactly 1 1/2" wide by about 3" long. It helps if one strip is lighter or darker than the other two. Using your machine's 1/4" guide, very carefully sew these three strips together side-by-side with the contrasting strip in the center. Now, measure the width of the center strip; it should be exactly 1" wide. If not, then you need to create a new, more accurate 1/4" guide for your machine.

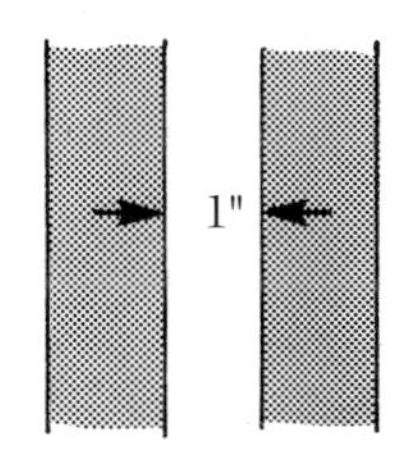

After you sew the three 1 1/2" strips together side by side, the center strip should measure a perfect 1" from seam to seam.

If the center strip is wider than 1", then the seam was too narrow, and the guide needs to be adjusted to the right. If the strip is less than 1", which is usually the case, then the seam is too large, and the guide needs to be made smaller by moving it to the left.

Adjusting the Seam Guide

If you have a machine with adjustable needle positions, try shifting your needle one notch to the right to create a smaller seam and to the left to sew a larger seam. One notch to the right is perfect for Berninas and some other brands. Remember that a straight-stitch throat plate cannot be used if the needle is not in its center position.

If the machine's needle is not adjustable, try a different presser foot; it may produce the results you need. One of my former students came up with an extremely innovative solution. She took her presser foot to a machine shop and had it filed down to the exact size she needed!

If you cannot adjust your needle or change presser feet to suit your needs, you will have to create your own masking-tape guide on the throat plate of your machine. This is not difficult to accomplish. First, raise the presser foot and lower the needle. Align the 1/4" guide of a ruler or piece of graph paper (1/8" or 1/4" grid) just to the left of the needle. If using graph paper, put the unthreaded needle into the paper just to the right of the 1/4" grid line so the needle is included in the 1/4" area.

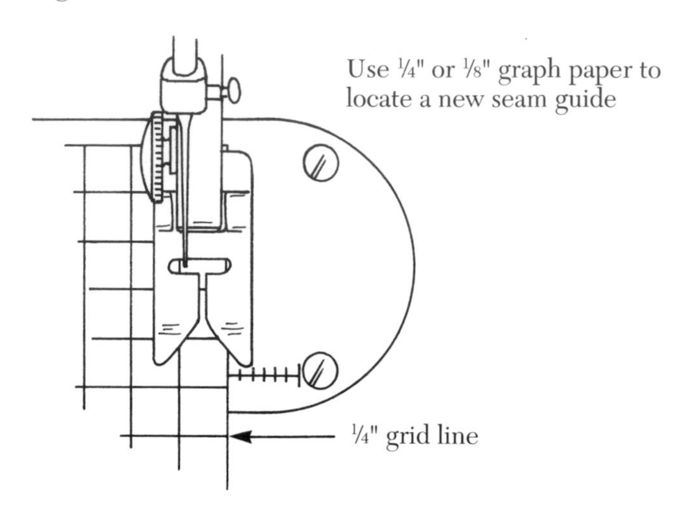

Use 1/4" or 1/8" graph paper to locate a new seam guide

Place a masking-tape guide on the throat plate along the right edge of the ruler or graph paper. Adjust the masking-tape guide so that it is running straight down from the needle and not canted to either the left or the right.

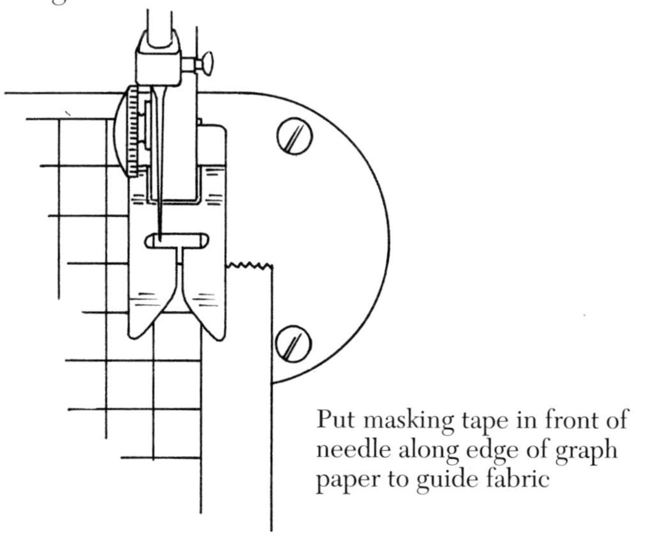

Put masking tape in front of needle along edge of graph paper to guide fabric

Cut a new set of 1 1/2" strips and try the strip test again with the new 1/4" guide. Keep adjusting and testing the guide until you are able to produce a perfect 1" strip every time. You must have an extremely accurate seam gauge for the miniatures to fit together. There is not much room for error on such tiny pieces, so take the time now to set up a proper gauge. Once you have the proper mark, it can be built up with several layers of tape or a piece of moleskin to better guide the fabric edge.

Stitch Size

Since the finished dimension of most of the units in these miniature quilts is only 1/4"–3/8", the stitch length must be adjusted accordingly. If you set your machine to a traditional 10 stitches per inch, you will have only 2 1/2–3 1/2 stitches to a seam. Instead, set your machine at 15 stitches per inch to safely accommodate the size of the pieces you are assembling. I set my Bernina stitch gauge at 1 3/4.

Sewing Speed

If you have a machine that has a half-speed setting, it's a good idea to engage that little gadget. If not, you must make a conscious effort to sew slowly. There is no substitute for slow and steady when working with miniatures. The quilt pieces are small, and mistakes are easily made if you try to zip along at a merry pace.

Needle Position

Always stop the machine with the needle in the down position. Again, it's helpful if you have a machine that can be set to do this automatically. When you are chain sewing or lifting the presser foot, the needle will keep the tiny pieces from shifting out of position.

Starting and Stopping with a Fabric Scrap

I picked up this wonderful tip in a workshop given by Jeannette Muir. Whether working on miniatures or not, this technique may well become a favorite.

Begin a line of sewing by first stitching completely across a folded scrap strip of fabric (about 1"–2" wide). Leave the needle down in the forward edge of the strip and do not lift the presser foot. Clip the thread tails. Now position the seam to be sewn under the presser foot just in front of the strip and begin sewing normally. I save strips left over from strip piecing in a basket near my machine for exactly this purpose.

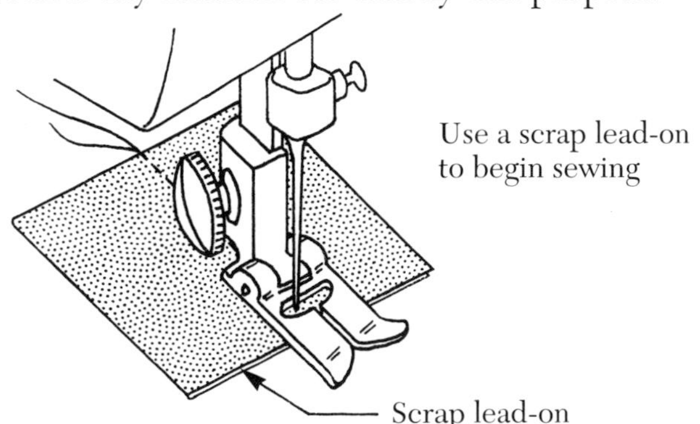

In the same manner, when you have finished a seam or stretch of chain sewing, run a scrap lead-off under the needle without lifting either the needle or presser foot. Remove your sewn seam from the other side of the needle and presser foot by clipping the little thread chain connecting it to the scrap lead-off. Your machine is now ready for whatever you have to sew next. The scrap lead-off becomes the next seam's scrap lead-on. Use the scrap leads over and over until they are completely filled with stitching before discarding them.

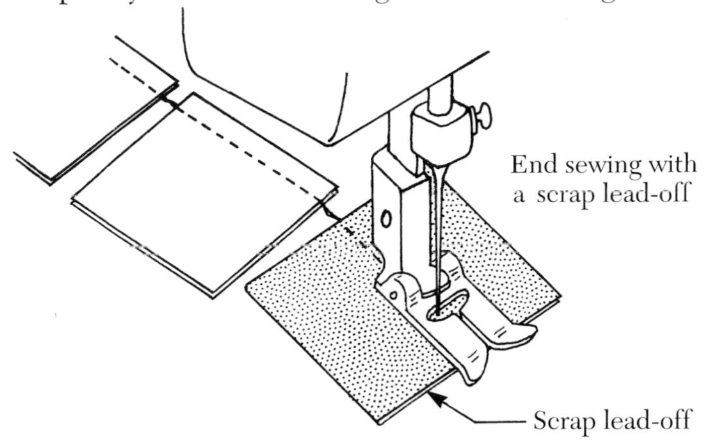

There are several advantages to this scrap lead-on/off technique. First of all, there are no longer thousands of little thread tails all over your sewing area or hanging from your seam ends. This means less thread waste, too.

Secondly, the scrap lead-on can help alleviate fabric "eating," which is a problem with some machines. Having fabric between the feed dog and presser foot in the area behind the needle seems to help the machine feed the small pieces through more smoothly. This advantage will be lost, though, if you use fabric that is a different weight from what you are sewing.

I've also noticed that some machines produce rough stitches at the beginning of a seam. The scrap lead-on harmlessly absorbs these stitches and allows the machine to sew a better quality seam where it counts.

Lifting the Presser Foot

Whenever a seam is begun, the top fabric runs the risk of being pushed forward ever so slightly by the presser foot. Usually on full-size quilts this movement is not a major problem. If it does cause problems, the quilter can shift the top fabric slightly ahead of the bottom fabric. However, with miniatures, there isn't as much room for this kind of guesswork, so it is wise to lift the presser foot slightly to properly place each unit under the needle before sewing. It is an easily acquired habit that I encourage you to develop.

The Better Finger

Often, with miniatures, your fingers are bigger than the pieces of fabric you are trying to guide under the needle. Try using a seam ripper as a "better finger" to guide the fabric right up to the needle. It can hold intersections together with pinpoint accuracy and make minute adjustments in shifting fabric that fingers simply can't handle. The seam ripper also is less likely to stretch the fabric while sewing. By substituting a seam ripper for your fingers, you'll find you will have a lighter but more accurate touch.

Chain Sewing

Chain sewing is an assembly-line approach to machine piecing. The idea is to save time by sewing as many seams as possible, one right after the other, rather than stopping and starting after each unit is sewn.

Begin a stretch of chain sewing with the scrap lead-on, followed by the first unit. Stop at the edge of the finished seam and don't raise the needle, lift the presser foot, or remove the finished unit from the machine.

Prepare the next unit for sewing, lift the presser foot slightly, and slip it underneath, leaving a small gap between the sewn unit and the new unit. Lower the presser foot and continue sewing.

Continue in this same fashion with all the units, ending with a scrap lead-off. Clip the chain from the back of the lead-off, leaving the lead-off in the machine for your next stretch of sewing. You should now have a long "kite tail" of sewn units connected by small twists of thread. These units may now be clipped apart. You are now ready to sew the next batch of units, with no thread tails cluttering your work area.

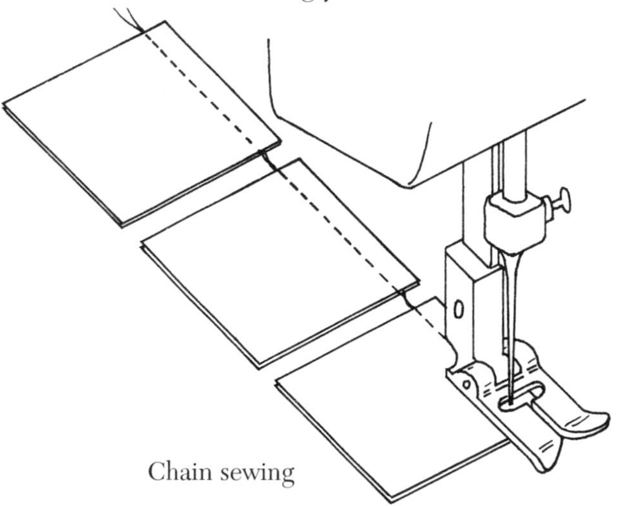

Chain sewing

Trimming the Seam Allowance

Once a seam is sewn it must be checked for accuracy. Make sure you have joined the correct edges together and sewn the correct-size seam. Once you are certain the seam is accurate, it must be trimmed to 1/8" before sewing any further. It is difficult to trim a seam once it has been crossed by the next seam. Make it a habit to check and trim after each seam is sewn. Instructions to trim the seams to 1/8" are not repeated throughout the patterns. It is assumed that you will remember to do this on your own.

Pressing Seams

When several tiny strips or units are being sewn together side by side, the work to the left of the needle must lie as flat as possible so that it can travel under the presser foot unimpeded. A series of 1/8"–1/4" unpressed strips will bump the presser foot around, resulting in an uneven, inaccurate seam. Therefore, each seam must be pressed as soon as it has been sewn, checked, and trimmed.

The guidelines for pressing are the same for miniatures as they are for full-size quilts. Preplan how you will press your seams throughout the block so that bulk is evenly distributed and your block assembles easily. It is of the utmost importance to press seams so they will form intersections in opposite directions to ease sewing and distribute bulk. This will be discussed further in the next section: Stitching Tips.

Keep in mind the following hints when pressing seams.

1. Most seam allowances will fall toward the area of least piecing. It's wise to accommodate this tendency, although every rule has its exceptions.
2. If possible, press seams toward the darker fabric in the seam to avoid having the dark fabric show through the lighter fabric.
3. At points where several seams meet in one place, try pressing all the seams in a circular clockwise fashion.
4. Sometimes, the best possible way to handle the seams is to press them open. This is a last resort, though, as an open seam is weaker and can provide a place for batting to pull through. Even though miniature seams are only 1/8", they still occupy a large portion of the area under a design. In the interest of flatness, there are times when you may have to choose an open seam over the alternatives.
5. Try not to press more than one or two seams inward on any single triangle.
6. If you will be joining quilt blocks to each other without sashing, it is very important to plan the seam allowance directions beforehand so that the blocks will join together easily.
7. When seaming two bias squares together, the diagonal seam allowances that lie on top of each other should be pressed in opposite directions. The diagonal seams will then butt against each other, making for well-matched points where they meet at the seam.

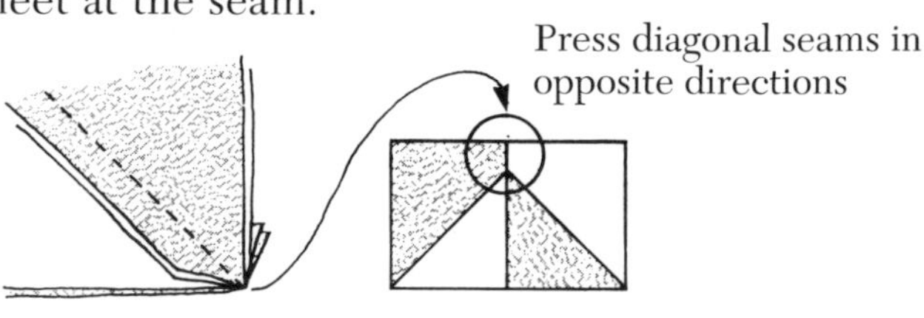

Press diagonal seams in opposite directions

8. When joining a strip of bias squares together for a border, as in the Churn Dash quilt on page 52, stitch bias squares to form pairs. Use two bias squares with seams pressed in opposite directions for each pair. Stitch pairs together and press as shown in diagram.

9. If you need to change the direction of an already pressed seam, first press the seam allowance back to its original unpressed position and steam it. A particularly recalcitrant seam can be coaxed into cooperation with a fine spray from a mister. Be careful not to stretch or pull on the fabric when pressing it. Once the seam is flat and the wrong pressing line ironed out, re-press it in the new direction.

Stitching Tips

In addition to the basic concepts of accurately aligning raw edges and sewing a consistently straight seam, there are a few extra tips to help your stitching progress smoothly.

1. Use a seam ripper or similar slender pointed device to gently guide your work (see The Better Finger section beginning on page 19). Be aware of where the bias edges are and do not tug or stretch on these edges at any time, particularly while sewing.
2. Butt opposing seam allowances against each other to form highly accurate intersections. Whenever possible, sew such an intersection with the raw edge of the top seam allowance heading toward the needle. The tendency of the top layer of fabric to be pushed forward will ensure a tight intersection since the top layer will be forced into the ridge of the bottom layer.

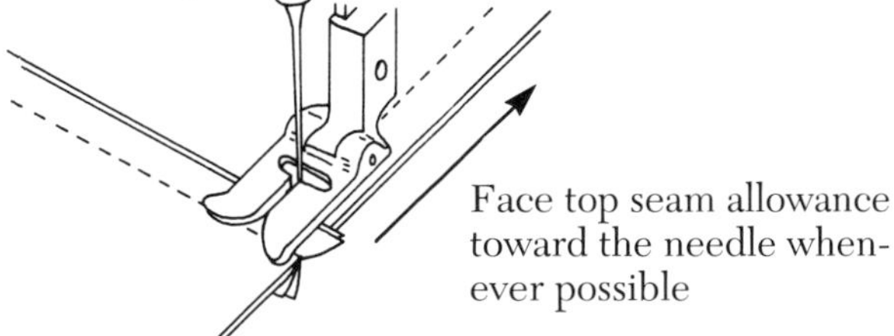

Face top seam allowance toward the needle whenever possible

When the raw edge of the top seam is facing away from the needle, it can be further pushed away from the intersection by the presser foot. In this situation, it is best to place the seam ripper against the upper seam while gently holding the lower layer in place. In this manner, the intersection can be secured until it is sewn in place.

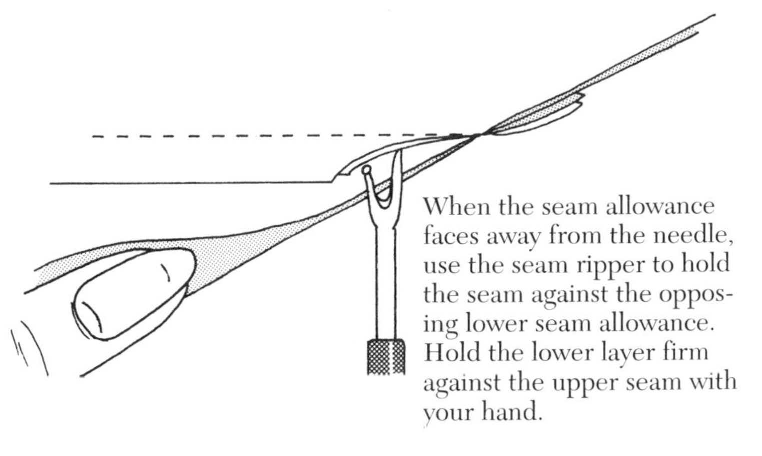

When the seam allowance faces away from the needle, use the seam ripper to hold the seam against the opposing lower seam allowance. Hold the lower layer firm against the upper seam with your hand.

3. When sewing a series of units together side by side, do not first sew them into pairs and then join the pairs. It is much easier to build the series one unit at a time from left to right. The presser foot will travel more easily over a smooth, unpieced top fabric than a lumpy, multiseamed unit. Place your fingers on the work just to the left of the presser foot to help keep the layers flat as they pass between the feed dog and presser foot. Again, be careful not to tug on the fabric as it travels or you may distort the sewing line. If you were to attempt to sew with a multipieced unit on top, the exposed seam allowances would cause the presser foot to jump and shift as it hit them. There are times when you will have to work with many seams exposed on top. At these times, you must sew very, very slowly and press the work as flat as possible while it is moving. Sometimes a piece of stiff paper between the left side of the presser foot and the seams can help smooth the ride.
4. When sewing a long seam that crosses over several other seams that need to match, match and sew just to the first intersection and lock it in place with a stitch. Before proceeding, butt the seams of the next intersection and use your seam ripper to hold it secure as it moves up to the needle. Use this point-to-point system for sewing all the intersections along the entire length of the seam.

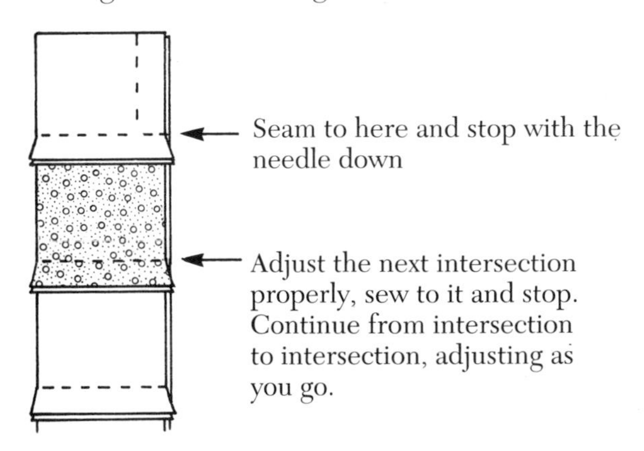

5. When triangles are sewn together, the intersecting sewing lines form an X at the seam line. This X can be used as a guide for sewing any subsequent crossover seams.

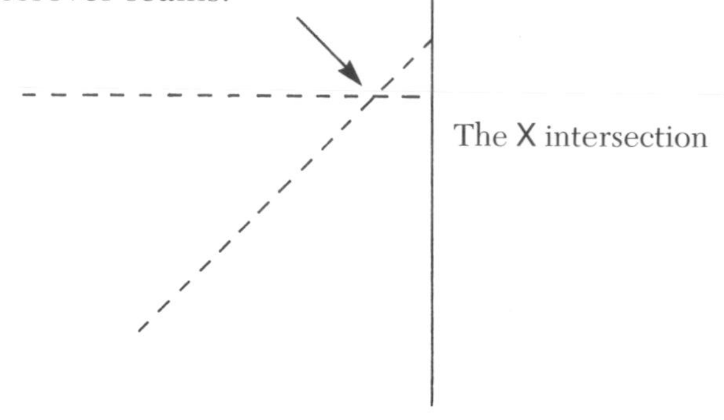

6. After you have completed a unit or block, it is a good idea to "true up" the edges. Use your rulers to check the dimensions of each actual block or unit against the theoretical size (don't forget to include the outside seam allowances). Make sure that the distance from a triangle point to the raw edge is ¼". Check all other reference points in the same fashion. The diagonal line on the Bias Square® is extremely helpful in checking anything with a diagonal arrangement. By checking these things now, you'll be able to make adjustments and accommodations as necessary and avoid surprises later.
7. When sewing individual triangles to another unit, such as a square, always sew the seam from the right-angle side of the triangle, not the point. If the triangle point is oversized and stretches, the excess can be trimmed away at a later time . This can't be done if you sew from the point first.

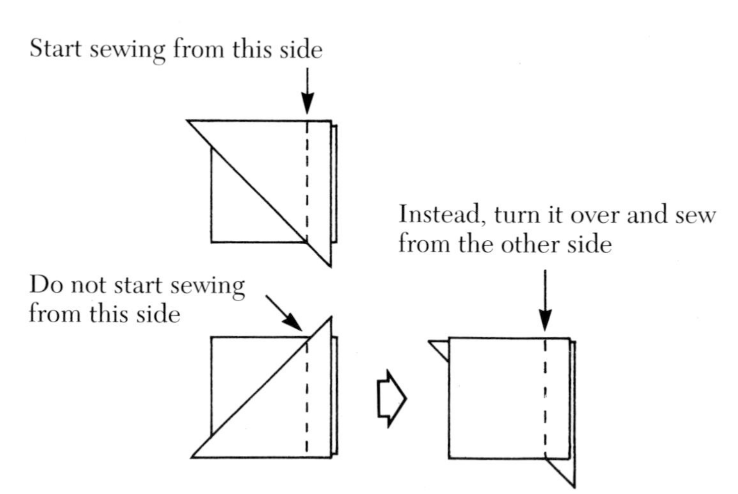

8. When sewing two units together that do not quite match, stitch with the fuller piece on the bottom. The feed dog of the sewing machine will ease in small amounts of excess fullness.

QUILT TOP ASSEMBLY

There is nothing unusual about the way miniatures are assembled into quilts. All the same principles that apply to full-size quilts hold for miniatures. Blocks are assembled by joining smaller units into larger units and then joining these to form the blocks. Some of the quilts in this book have straight-set blocks and some have a diagonal set. You will also find sets with sashing and those without. Assembly instructions are given with each pattern.

Sashing

When assembling a quilt with sashing, make sure that the sashes joining blocks together align with each other to create a continuous visual line. First, join the blocks with the short sashes to form rows. Add a long sash to the bottom of the row. On the wrong side of the bottom sash, make pencil marks on the raw edge indicating where interior seams of the short sashings would fall if they extended all the way to the edge.

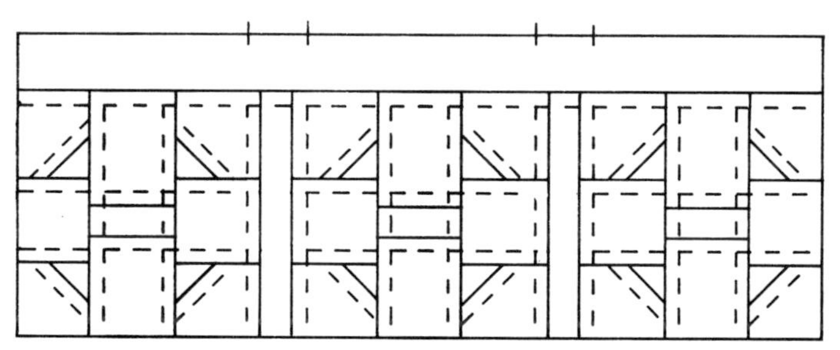

Make marks on the raw edge of the long sashing where the short sashing seams lie

Now, join the first row and its lower sash to the second row by aligning the pencil marks with the sashing seams of the second row. Join all the rows in this fashion.

Borders

The edges of a quilt should be straightened before the borders are added. There will probably be little or nothing to trim on a straight-set quilt. A diagonal-set quilt is often constructed with oversized side triangles and these need to be trimmed back. Align the ¼" ruler guide along the block points and trim the quilt edges to ¼" from these reference points. Always have a ruler guide along the block points of the adjacent edge so that the corner will be square when the trimming is done.

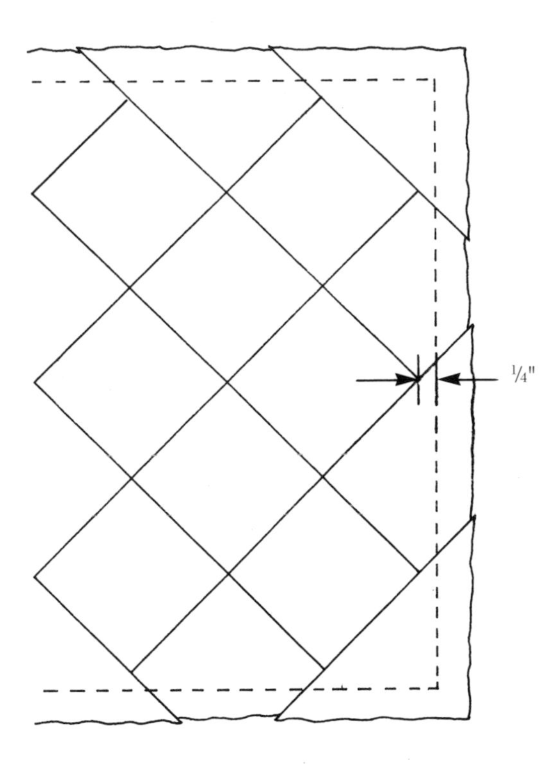

Trim the edges of the quilt to 1/4" from the block points

Most of the patterns in this book have straight-set borders. Those with pieced borders have specific border assembly instructions, which are optional. Please feel free to substitute plain borders in lieu of any of the fancy borders presented. In fact, feel free to change any part of any pattern to make the quilt your own!

To find the correct measurement for the border strips, always measure through the center of the quilt, not at the edges. This ensures that the borders are of equal size and the outer edges brought into line with the center dimension if discrepancies exist.

For straight-set borders, measure the quilt from top to bottom through the center of the quilt. Cut two of the border strips to this measurement and sew to the sides of the quilt, adjusting the quilt to fit the border length. Press the seams toward the border strips. After the sides are attached, measure the width of the quilt top through the center, including the two side border strips. Cut the other two strips to this measurement and sew them to the top and bottom of the quilt top. Press the seams toward the border strips.

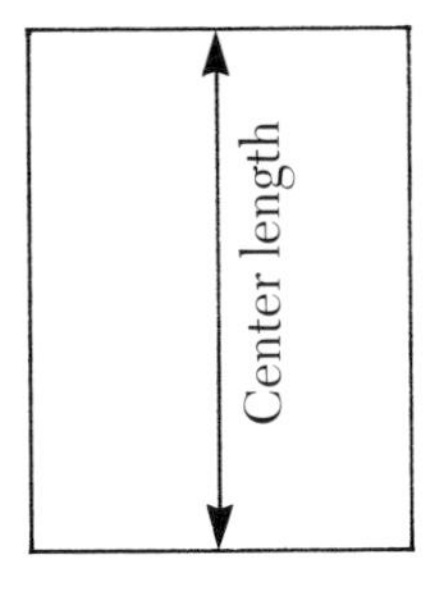

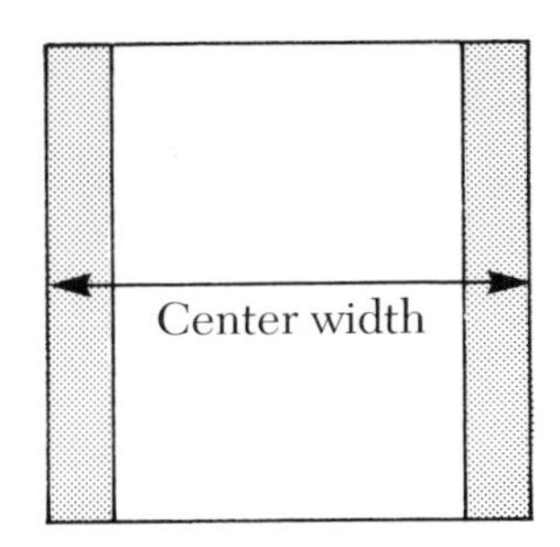

For straight-set borders, first measure through the center length and cut side borders to this measurement; seam them to the sides. Then, measure through the new center width and cut the top and bottom borders to this measurement; seam them to the top and bottom.

If there are cornerstones, measure all four border strips before attaching the sides. Attach the cornerstones to the top and bottom strips, then sew these strips to the quilt last.

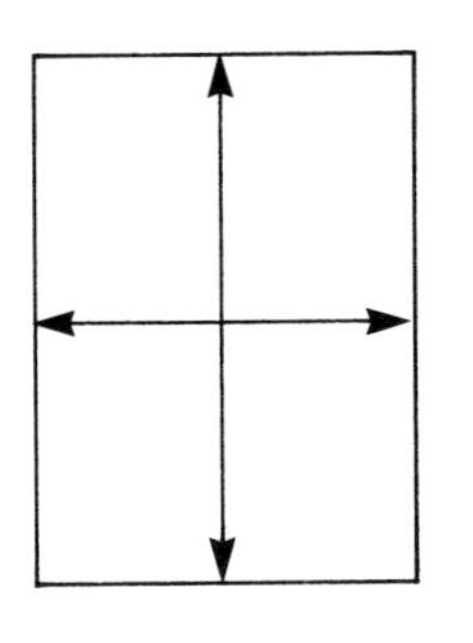

For borders with cornerstones, first measure all borders through the center width or length of unfinished quilt top

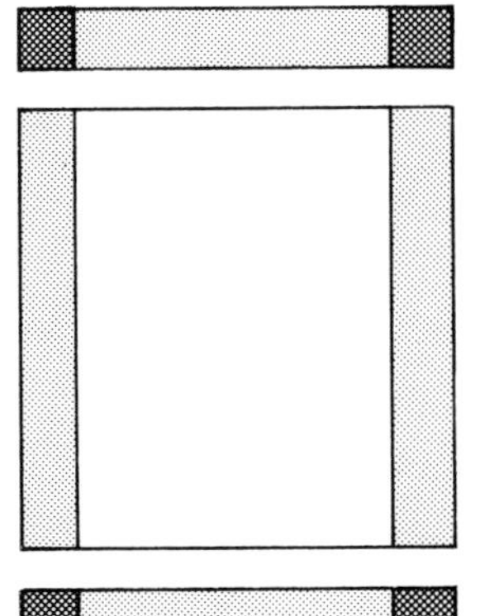

Add the side borders to the quilt. Add the cornerstones to the top and bottom strips before adding them to the quilt.

Gallery of Quilts

Tulips *by Donna Lynn Thomas, 1989, Broomall, Pennsylvania, 6¾" x 8¾". The outer border ties together an assortment of solid pastels in this pretty springtime quilt.*

Album Quilt *by Donna Lynn Thomas, 1988, Frankfurt, West Germany, 10½" x 12". The fabrics for this quilt were chosen to complement the border print. True to tradition, the names of family members and friends are written in the center of each block.*

Sister's Choice *by Donna Lynn Thomas, 1990, Frankfurt, West Germany, 8½" x 8½". The black and fuchsia prints create a strong contrast for this small quilt. Try substituting Snowball blocks for the plain blocks to produce a striking overall design.*

Stars and Wheels *by Donna Lynn Thomas, 1989, Broomall, Pennsylvania, 8" x 8". This quilt, made just for the fun of a challenge, consists of four Variable Stars surrounded by a Pinwheel border. There are 448 triangles (224 bias squares) in the 56 scrap Pinwheels surrounding the center.*

Fire and Ice *by Donna Lynn Thomas, 1990, Frankfurt, West Germany, 14" x 14". Two blocks, Spinning Star and Snowball, in icy blue and fiery red create an exciting overall design.*

Birds in the Air *by Donna Lynn Thomas, 1989, Frankfurt, West Germany, 6½" x 6½". This pattern is a wonderful way to use scraps—even in miniature!*

Sister's Choice *by Donna Lynn Thomas, 1989, Frankfurt, West Germany, 8½" x 12½". A full-sized quilt made by Sallie Jeannette Wilson and presented in the book* Women and Their Quilts, *by Nancyann Johanson Twelker (That Patchwork Place, Inc.), inspired this miniature quilt. The monochromatic color scheme leaves a soft, cool impression.*

Peony *by Donna Lynn Thomas, 1990, Frankfurt, West Germany, 12" x 14¾". Modeled after the traditional North Carolina Lily, this quilt evokes memories of colonial homes and times. The scalloped and appliquéd borders provide an interesting finish to a pretty design.*

Jacob's Ladder *by Donna Lynn Thomas, 1989, Frankfurt, West Germany, 15½" x 15½". Strong colors and an unusual block-to-block set creates the bold central design.*

***Indian Hatchet** by Donna Lynn Thomas, 1989, Frankfurt, West Germany, 5" x 7". Charming in miniature, this quilt works up quickly.*

***Shoo-Fly** by Donna Lynn Thomas, 1989, Frankfurt, West Germany, 5¾" x 7⅜". The traditional red-and-green colors combine with this old-fashioned block to make a charming miniature quilt.*

***Inside-Outside Stars** by Donna Lynn Thomas, 1989, Broomall, Pennsylvania, 10" x 10". The pieced border surrounding the scrappy Variable Stars is a simple but exciting addition to a lively quilt.*

Delectable Mountains *by Donna Lynn Thomas, 1989, Frankfurt, West Germany, $10\frac{1}{4}$" x $10\frac{1}{4}$". Originally pieced in cherry red and cream, this quilt was heavily tea-dyed to create an antique look.*

Old-time Alphabet *by Donna Lynn Thomas, 1990, Frankfurt, West Germany, $8\frac{1}{2}$" x 10". The alphabet quilt, a design from days gone by, is reproduced here in deep purple, brick, and pale green.*

Making the Quilts Section I:

As I reviewed the patterns for this book, it seemed logical to arrange them in order from simplest to most difficult so that a quilter would have an idea of the level of difficulty she was attempting. The quilts also fell easily into three categories: strip piecing, bias squares, and side-by-side triangles. Within each category, there were also two sizes of quilt blocks, those based on a ⅜" subunit and those based on a ¼" subunit. Therefore, this part of the book is divided into three sections in order of increasing difficulty. Each section begins with information on the specific skills required to complete the quilts that follow, along with a warm-up project that enables you to master those skills before moving on to the patterns. The warm-up projects are not as small as the quilt patterns so that you may move gradually from the world of full-size blocks to miniatures. I encourage you to work with the warm-up project in each section until you feel you have mastered its skills. Then, you can confidently progress to the patterns, which are also arranged from simplest to most complex.

The list of fabrics in each pattern describes the fabrics used in the photograph model. Unless you are duplicating the model exactly, it's helpful to make a swatch card listing your personal fabric choices and their corresponding fabric numbers. On a 3" x 5" card, list the fabrics called for in the pattern. Then, tape or glue a small swatch of your choice for that fabric next to the number. In this way, you have a personal reference to use when reading pattern instructions.

I have tried to eliminate repetitive instructions and am assuming that you will automatically check the accuracy of each seam as you finish it. I am also assuming that you will know to trim each seam to ⅛" after it has been checked. Please keep these two items in mind as you work.

When you have completed your quilt top, please turn to Finishing Up, page 82, for information on how to finish it into a miniature quilt.

STRIPS AND SNOWBALLS

The concept of quick piecing not only enables one to make quilt tops more quickly but also to make them more accurately. Traditional construction steps are frequently combined, sometimes eliminated, and occasionally rearranged in sequence. Section I deals with the simplest of the concepts—strip piecing and Snowballs.

Strata Assembly

A strata is a series of strips sewn together side by side and then cut into segments to produce presewn units. Success is ensured by accurately measuring, cutting, and sewing the strips.

Prepare your fabric for cutting as outlined in Basic Skills, page 14. The patterns in *Small Talk* already include the seam allowance in the cutting requirements so there is no need to do any additional figuring. Cut the strips required for the pattern according to the instructions for Cutting Strips, page 15, being careful to exactly align the proper ruler marking with the edge of the fabric. Before sewing the strips together side by side to form the strata, lay them next to each other in the order to be assembled. The pattern will have a diagram of each strata, including the cut dimensions and fabric identification of each strip.

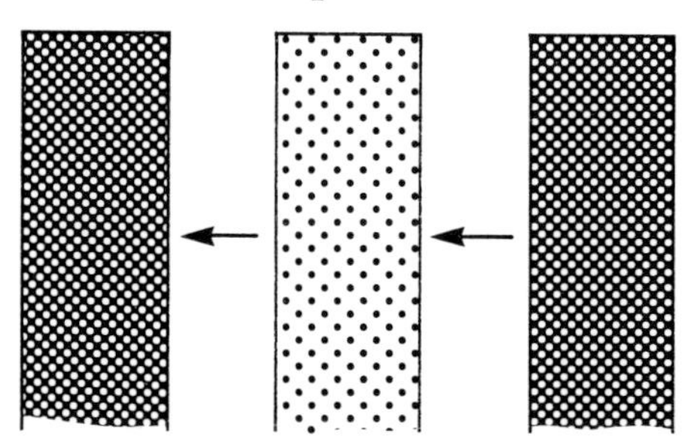

Pick up the two strips to the left and lay them right sides together. Using the proper ¼" seam guide, sew the seam connecting the two strips. Begin and end with a scrap lead-on/lead-off.

Check to make sure the correct seam is sewn (you'd be surprised how often even the most experienced quiltmaker will sew the wrong side!) and then trim it to ⅛". Press the seam to one side as outlined in the pattern or in your own preplanned pressing guide. Continue building the strata one strip at a time.

Cutting Segments

Turn the strata sideways so that one short end can be "trued up." Lay a horizontal ruler line on one of the seam lines near the short edge of the strata. If the seams are straight, they should all align with or be parallel to a ruler line. Keeping everything in line, move the ruler up to the edge of the strata and cut off any unevenness at the edge. Even if the edges are straight, it's a good idea to trim the ends to give a clean cut and eliminate any rough starts on the seams. This true edge is the guide you need to be able to make segment cuts at right angles to the seam.

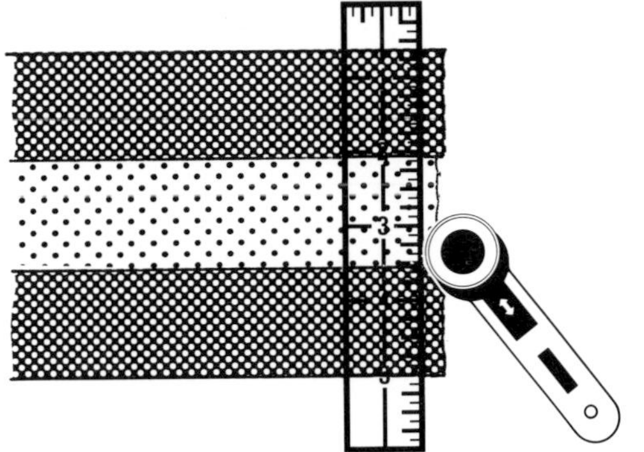

Once the strata end is trimmed, cut segments according to the pattern instructions. Beginning with the freshly cut strata end, measure in the prescribed distance for the segment. Never make a segment cut without also laying a horizontal ruler line on one of the interior seams. It is very important that the cut be at right angles to the seams. Ideally, the upper and lower raw edges should also align, but, if necessary, you can make adjustments when the final seams are sewn. An interior seam is already locked in and will appear slanted if the cut is not made at right angles to it.

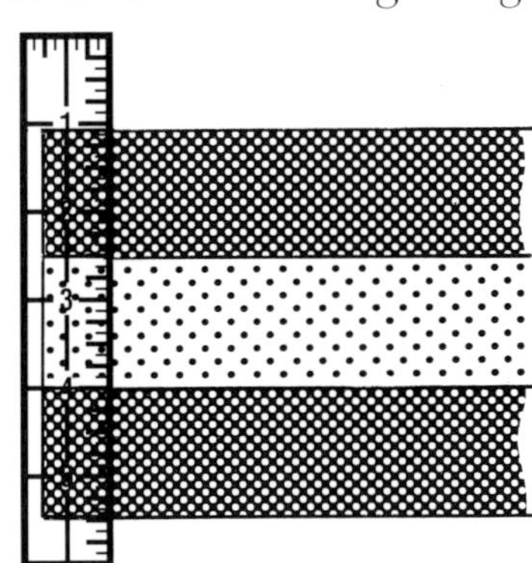

If, at any time, the short edge and interior seams no longer form a right angle, the edge needs to be trued up again. This happens periodically and is nothing to be alarmed about. It is due to the minuscule amount of ruler slippage that occurs with each cut. Of course, the more carefully you cut, the less frequently you will have to recut the edges. I have tried to incorporate extra length in the strata to account for this phenomenon.

These segments can be used and combined with other units in various ways to create different blocks. Each pattern will have specific instructions for the segments' use.

Creating Snowball Blocks

Snowball blocks are plain squares with the corners lopped off. Triangles of a different color or colors are then resewn onto the lopped-off corners.

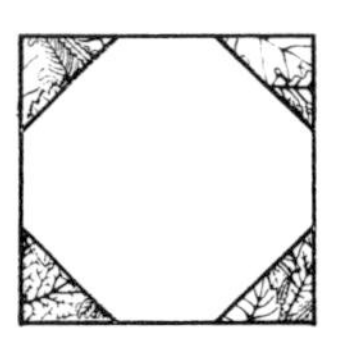

These blocks are favorites for two-block overall design quilts, such as Around the Twist (page 44) or Snow Patch (page 34). There are three steps involved in making Snowball blocks.

1. Create a template guide for cutting the corners off the original square. Trudie Hughes calls this guide a Speedy in her Template-Free™ series of books.
2. Determine the size triangle to resew back onto the corners. The new triangles are not the same size as the Speedy, so do not make the mistake of using it as a guide for this step.
3. Nub the points of the corner triangles so that they can be accurately sewn onto the square.

The patterns requiring a Snowball block provide the template of the Speedy needed but it's a good idea to know for yourself the simple methods used to create this versatile block.

Creating a Speedy

Method I:

Begin by drawing the finished size Snowball block on a piece of 1/8" graph paper. Now, draw 1/4" seam allowances along the two short sides of one of the corner triangles.

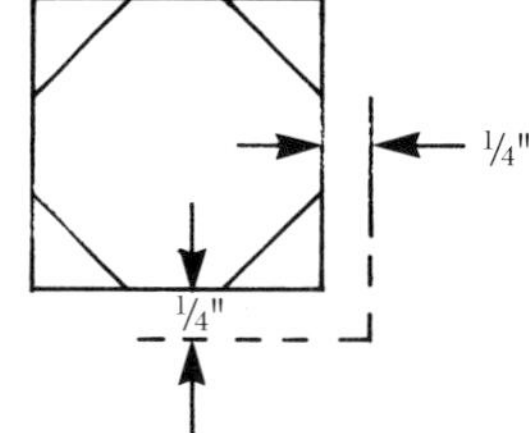

Next, draw a 1/4" seam allowance inside the long edge of the triangle. The new triangle formed is your Speedy.

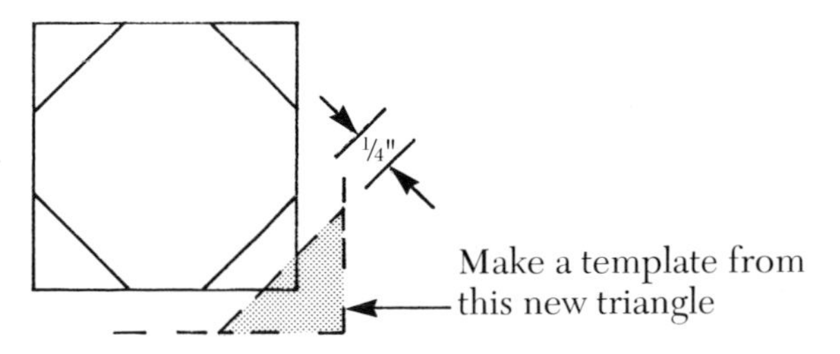

Method II:

A shortcut to all this drawing is to determine the finished size of the corner to be removed and add 1/8" to this figure. Draw a triangle this size for the Speedy. For example, if the corner to be removed is 1/2" in finished size, the Speedy would be 5/8" (4/8" + 1/8" = 5/8").

No matter which method you use, make an accurate plastic template of the Speedy triangle. Tape this little piece of plastic to the edge of your ruler with the long edge of the Speedy precisely aligned with the edge of the ruler. Try to use a section of the ruler where there is a high degree of visibility.

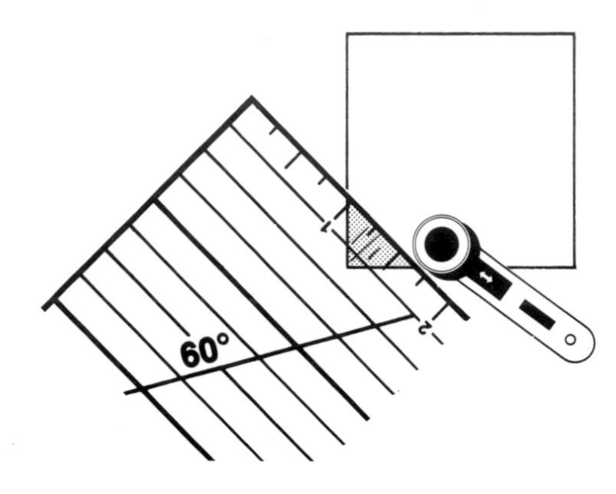

You now have a little guide on your ruler to exactly lop off the corners of the Snowball squares. Lay the corner of the Speedy over the corner of the square and cut along the long edge, using the edge of the ruler as the cutting guide.

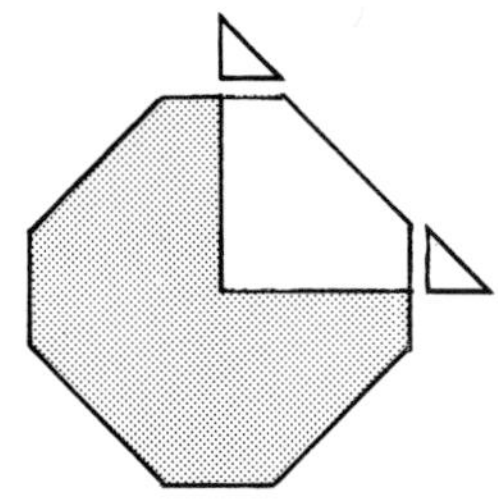

Determining the New Triangle Size

The new triangles to be sewn onto the lopped corners are half-square triangles and are prepared according to the instructions in Basic Skills, page 16.

Nubbing Triangle Points

When you are sewing a triangle onto the corner of a square, it is helpful to trim the triangle points to fit the side of the square.

A simple little addition and your rotary cutter will create just what is needed. Add 1/2" to the finished dimension of the short side of the triangle. For example, if the finished size is 1/2", add 1/2" to the finished size to equal 1". Lay the 1" ruler marking on one of the short sides of the triangle and remove the excess to the right of the ruler. Turn the triangle and nub the other triangle point.

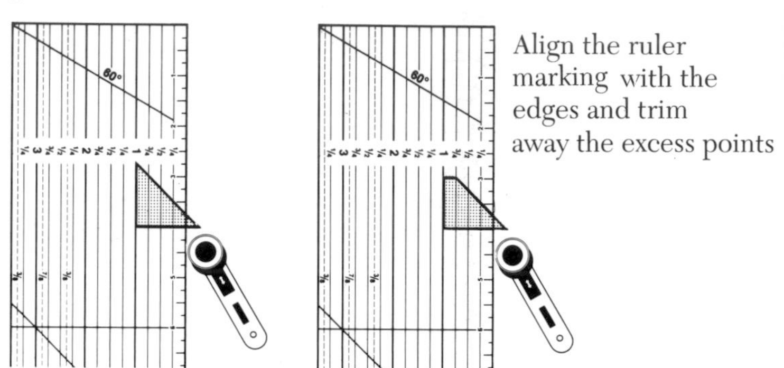

Align the ruler marking with the edges and trim away the excess points

The Bias Square® also can be used to nub the points of a triangle in this manner. Sew the nubbed triangles onto the lopped square to create the finished Snowball block.

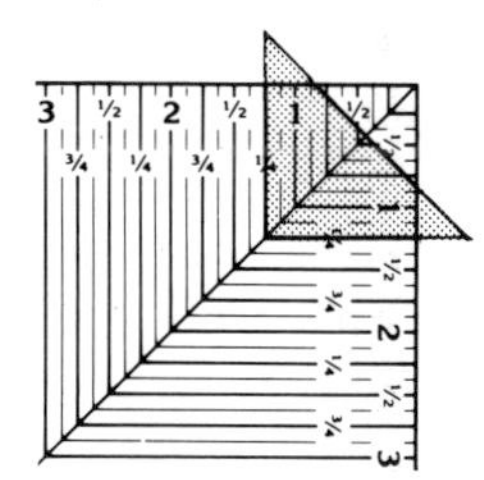

While assembling the warm-up project and patterns, be sure to always check your finished seams for accuracy before trimming them to 1/8" and proceeding.

Warm-Up Project: Snow Patch

$10\frac{3}{4}$" x $10\frac{3}{4}$"

The Snow Patch warm-up project alternates five Ninepatch blocks with four Snowball blocks to create a lovely overall design. It is a wonderful project for learning the basics of strip piecing and Snowball construction. Before starting, read through the following instructions to get an idea of what you will be doing.

Ninepatch block
Finished size: $2\frac{1}{4}$"

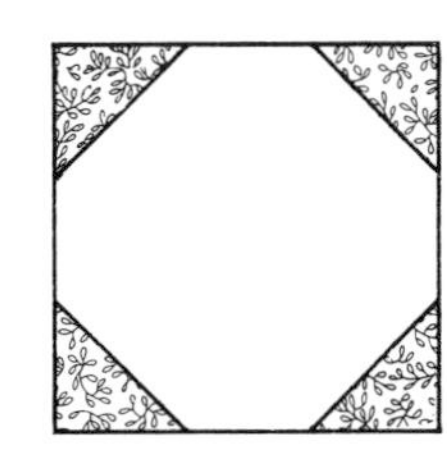

Snowball block
Finished size: $2\frac{1}{4}$"

Cutting Requirements

Fabric #1: Purple print, 12" x 16" piece
Cut:
- 2 strips, $1\frac{1}{4}$" x 15" (Strata I)
- 1 strip, $1\frac{1}{4}$" x $7\frac{1}{2}$" (Strata II)
- 2 strips, $1\frac{3}{4}$" x 13" (outer border)
- 2 strips, $1\frac{3}{4}$" x 9" (outer border)

Fabric #2: Peach print, 7" x 16" piece
Cut:
- 1 strip, $1\frac{1}{4}$" x 15" (Strata I)
- 2 strips, $1\frac{1}{4}$" x $7\frac{1}{2}$" (Strata II)
- 8 squares, $1\frac{5}{8}$" x $1\frac{5}{8}$" (Snowball corner triangles)

Fabric #3: Light peach solid, 9" x 13" piece
Cut:
- 4 squares, $2\frac{3}{4}$" x $2\frac{3}{4}$" (Snowball squares)
- 4 strips, 1" x 9" (inner border)

Backing and Binding: 12" square, your fabric choice. To mimic model, use Fabric #1 and a rolled binding (see page 84).

Assembly Instructions

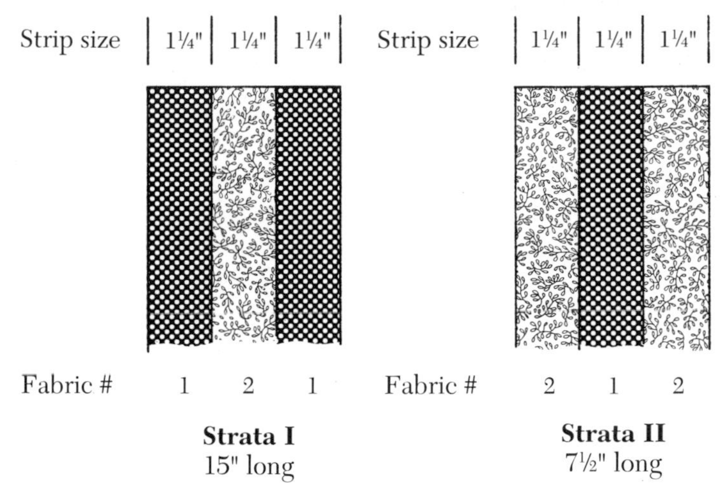

Strata I
15" long

Strata II
$7\frac{1}{2}$" long

1. Assemble Strata I and Strata II according to the diagrams. Press the seams in both strata toward the dark print.
2. Cut Strata I into $1\frac{1}{4}$" segments; cut 10. Cut Strata II into $1\frac{1}{4}$" segments; cut 5.
3. Lay the segments on the work area as in the diagram. Stack 5 segments in each pile.

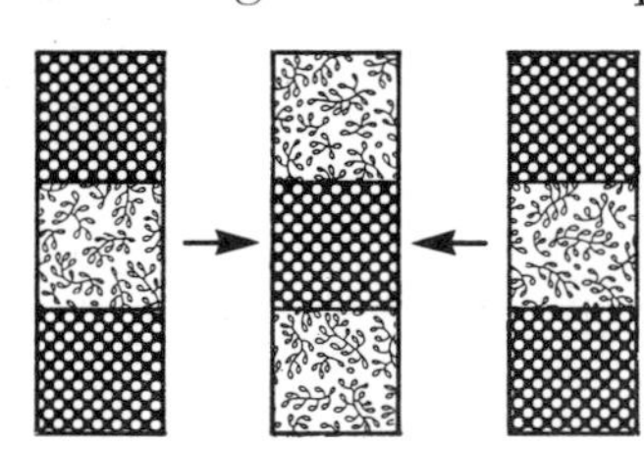

4. Chain sew all Strata II segments to the left-hand pile of Strata I segments.
5. Press the seams toward Strata I.
6. Add the last pile of Strata I segments to these new units.
7. Press the seams toward the outer edges of the blocks.
8. Make a plastic Speedy from the triangle in the diagram. It should measure $\frac{7}{8}$" on the short right-angle sides ($\frac{3}{4}$" finished size + $\frac{1}{8}$").

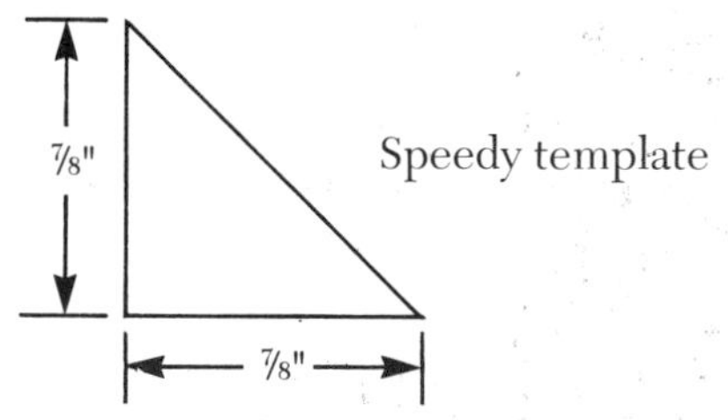

9. Tape the Speedy to your ruler, matching the long edge of the Speedy with the edge of the ruler. Cut off all 4 corners of the $2\frac{3}{4}$" Fabric #3 Snowball squares.
10. Cut the $1\frac{5}{8}$" Fabric #2 squares in half on the diagonal to form 16 right triangles. Nub the corners of

the triangles, following the instructions on page 32. **Hint:** The measuring guide will be 1$\frac{1}{4}$" since $\frac{3}{4}$" finished size + $\frac{1}{2}$" = 1$\frac{1}{4}$".

11. Sew a nubbed triangle to each corner of the Snowball squares and press the seams toward the center of the block.
12. Lay the Ninepatch blocks on the table alternately with the Snowball blocks as in the photograph. Align the intersections of the Snowball triangles and Ninepatch squares, using pins if necessary to hold them in place. Join the blocks into rows and press the seams toward the Snowball blocks.
13. Join the rows together to form the center body of the quilt top. Press the seams in either direction.
14. Following the directions for straight-set borders on page 23, attach the Fabric #3 inner border strips.
15. Attach the Fabric #1 outer border strips in the same fashion.
16. Quilt and bind as desired.

Snow Patch *by Donna Lynn Thomas, 1990, Frankfurt, West Germany, 10$\frac{3}{4}$" x 10$\frac{3}{4}$". The use of color and contrast help define this overall design. Quilted by Susan Stamilio.*

Rail Fence

13¼" x 13¼"

Strip piecing doesn't come any easier than this, whether one is working on a full-size quilt or a miniature. The success of the design comes in the choice of fabrics and the sewing of nice straight seams. Choose your fabrics so that they are graded in value from dark to light. This Rail Fence goes together quickly and makes a great break from other projects.

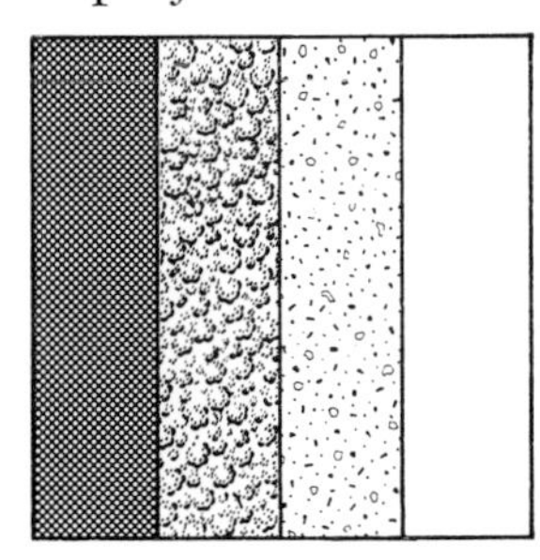

Rail Fence block
Finished size: 1½"

Cutting Requirements

Fabric #1: Dark pink print, 18" square
Cut: 4 strips, ⅞" x 15" (strata)
4 strips, 2½" x 11" (outer border)
4 squares, 2½" x 2½" (border corner squares)

Fabric #2: Medium pink print, 5" x 16" piece
Cut: 4 strips, ⅞" x 15" (strata)

Fabric #3: Pale green check, 5" x 16" piece
Cut: 4 strips, ⅞" x 15" (strata)

Fabric #4: Light print, 9" x 16" piece
Cut: 4 strips, ⅞" x 15" (strata)

Fabric #5: Dark teal print, 5" x 12" piece
Cut: 4 strips, 1" x 9" (inner border)
4 squares, 1" x 1" (border corner squares)

Backing and Binding: 13" x 16" piece, your fabric choice. To mimic model, use Fabric #5 and a rolled binding.

Assembly Instructions

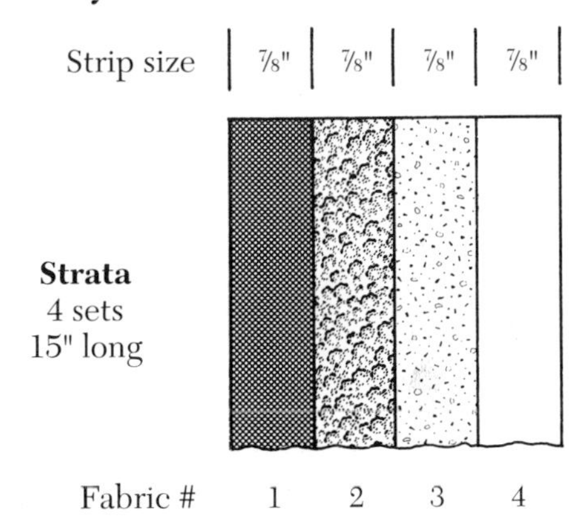

1. Assemble 4 sets of the strata. Press all seams toward the darker side. Cut sets into 2" segments. You will need 25.
2. Lay the segments on the work table as in the diagram.

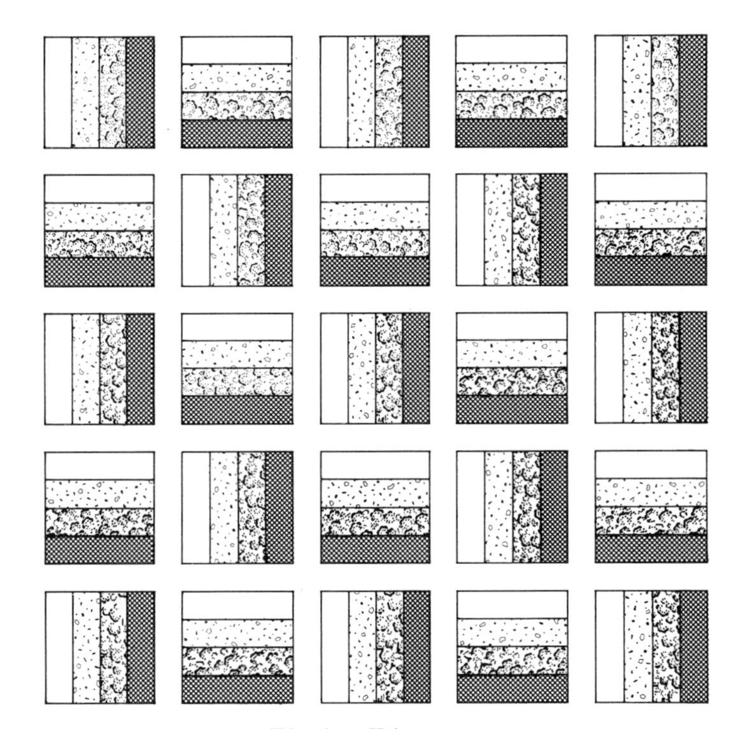

Piecing Diagram

3. Join the segments to form rows. Press the seams toward the vertical strips.
4. Join the rows to form the quilt top. Press the seams in either direction.

5. Following the directions for straight-set borders on page 23, attach the Fabric #5 inner border strips and cornerstones.
6. Attach the Fabric #1 outer border strips in the same fashion.
7. Quilt and bind as desired.

***Rail Fence** by Donna Lynn Thomas, 1990, Frankfurt, West Germany, 13¼" x 13¼". Pastels soften a definite linear design, resulting in a light and pretty quilt. Quilted by Ann Marie Eberlin.*

Double Irish Chain

10⅝" x 14⅜"

The Double Irish Chain quilt is a beloved traditional pattern that creates an appealing overall diagonal design. Depending on how the fabrics are used, you can accentuate either the squares running through the center of the chain or the squares running to either side. To give the center chain dominance (Fabric #1), try using a slightly lighter fabric for the outer chain (Fabric #2). Using a lighter fabric for Fabric #1 will give the two outer chains dominance. Choose your fabrics according to your preferences. The design is created by combining two pieced blocks. There are eight chain blocks (Block A) and seven pieced alternate blocks (Block B) that make up the quilt top.

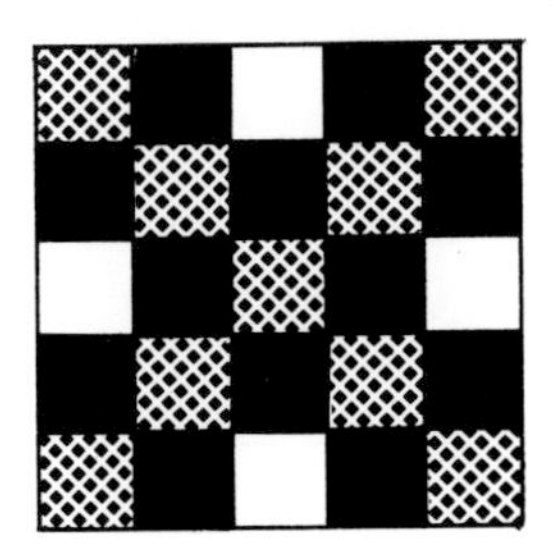

Irish Chain block
Block A
Finished size: 1⅞"

Alternate block
Block B
Finished size: 1⅞"

Cutting Requirements

Fabric #1: Red plaid, 12" x 18" piece
Cut:
4 strips, ⅞" x 17" (Strata I, Strata II)
1 strip, ⅞" x 9" (Strata III)
4 strips, ⅞" x 12" (middle border)

Fabric #2: Dark blue print, 19" square
Cut:
5 strips, ⅞" x 17" (Strata I, Strata II)
2 strips, ⅞" x 9" (Strata III)
2 strips, ⅞" x 15" (Strata IV)
4 strips 2¼" x 15" (outer border)

Fabric #3: Tea-dyed muslin, 9" x 18" piece
Cut:
1 strip, ⅞" x 17" (Strata I)
2 strips, ⅞" x 9" (Strata III)
1 strip, 1⅝" x 15" (Strata IV)
7 rectangles, 1⅝" x 2⅜" (Block B)

Fabric #4: Black solid, 5" x 11" piece
Cut:
4 strips, ⅞" x 12" (inner border)

Backing and Binding: 12" x 16" piece, your fabric choice. To mimic model, use Fabric #2 and a rolled binding.

Assembly Instructions

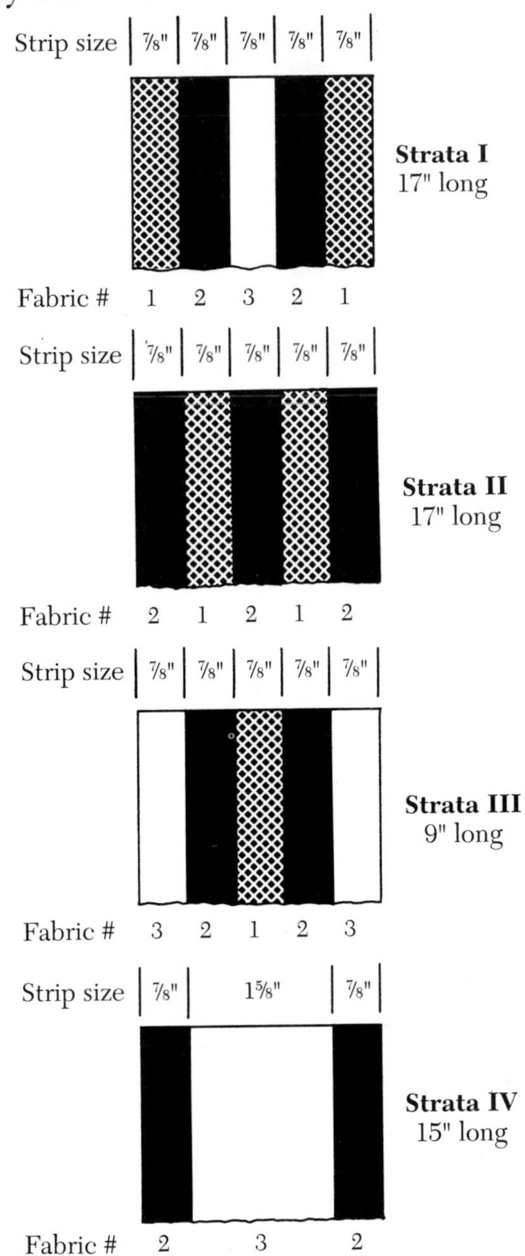

1. Assemble the 4 different sets of strata according to the diagram. Press the seams as follows:
   - Strata I: Press all seams away from center strip
   - Strata II: Press all seams toward center strip
   - Strata III: Press all seams away from center strip
   - Strata IV: Press all seams toward center strip
2. Cut strata into ⅞" segments as follows:
   - Strata I: 16
   - Strata II: 16
   - Strata III: 8
   - Strata IV: 14
3. Stack the segments from Strata I, II, and III on the work table as shown in the diagram. Join them

together one by one to form 8 Block A. Press all the seams away from the center segment.

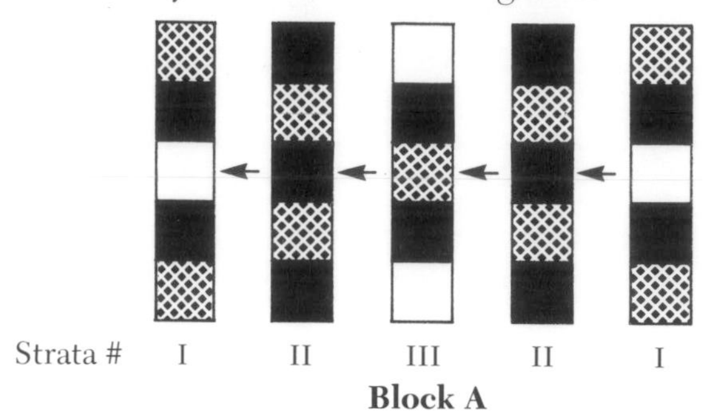

Block A

4. Lay the segments from Strata IV on either side of the 1⅝" x 2⅜" rectangles cut from Fabric #3. Join the three units together to form Block B; make 7 Block B. Press the seams toward the center.

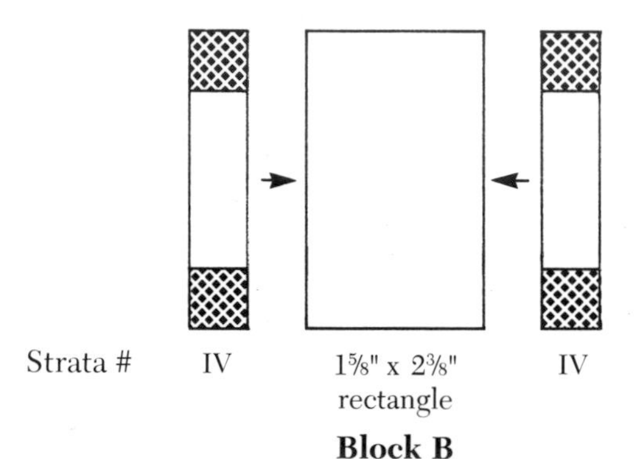

Block B

5. Arrange the blocks on the work table to form the quilt top. Be sure that the long seams of Block B run in the same direction consistently. Join the blocks to form rows and press the seams toward Block B. Assemble the rows to form the quilt top. Press the seams in either direction.

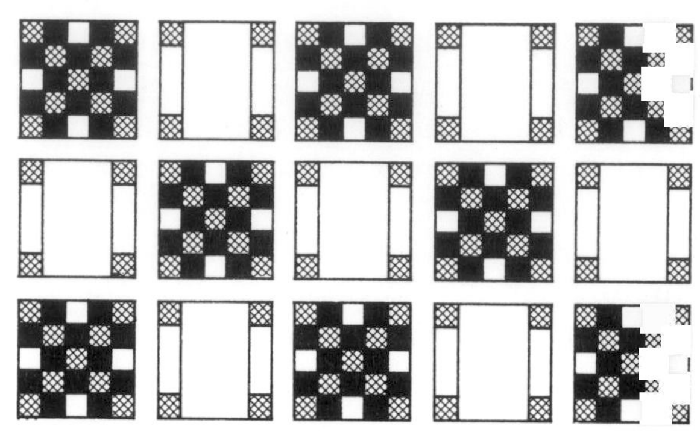

Piecing Diagram

6. Following the directions for straight-set borders on page 23, attach the Fabric #4 inner border strips.
7. Attach the middle and outer borders in the same fashion.
8. Quilt and bind as desired.

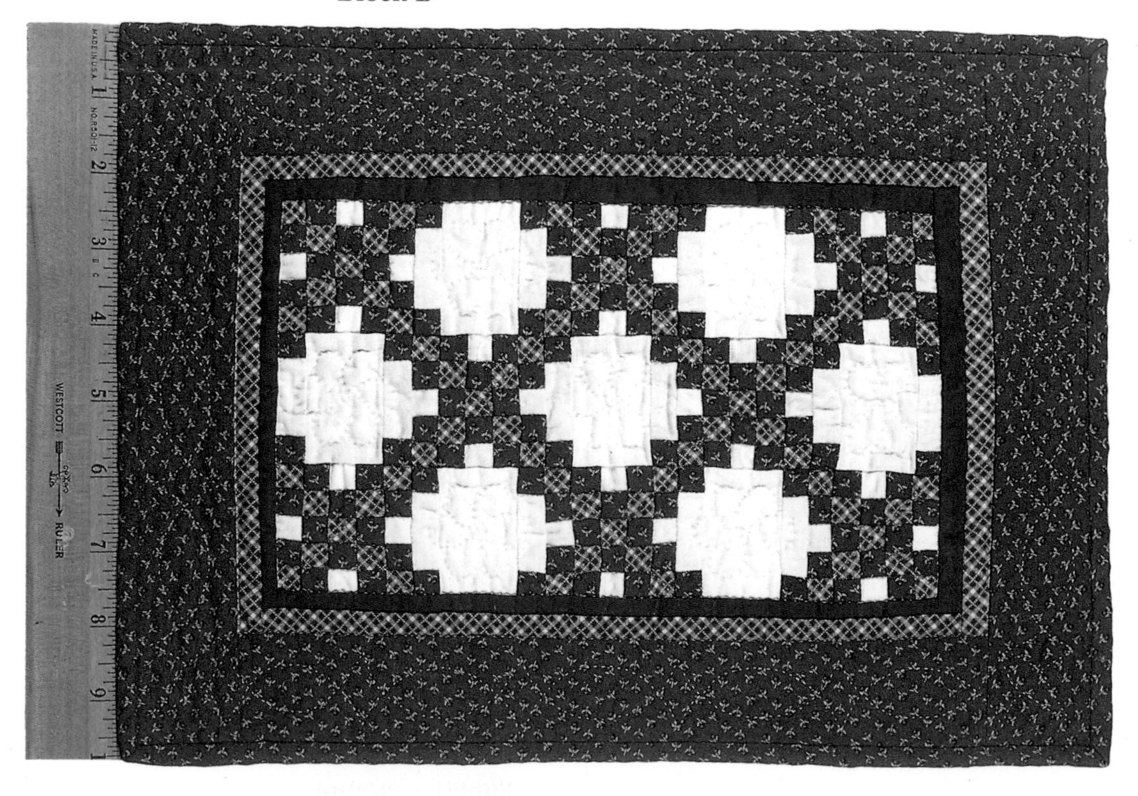

***Double Irish Chain** by Donna Lynn Thomas, 1987, Brookhaven, Pennsylvania, 10⅝" x 14⅜". What better way to recreate an old-fashioned quilt than with the tried-and-true color combination of red, tan, and blue?*

Cross-eyed Puss

9¾" x 9¾"

Cross-eyed Puss is another quilt that combines two different blocks, Cross and Puss-in-the-Corner, to create an overall design. Unlike the straight sets of the Ninepatch and Double Irish Chain quilts, the blocks are joined on the diagonal. To make this quilt, you will be assembling blocks based on ¼" subunits. The finished size of each block is only 1" but is relatively simple to construct. In addition to the two main blocks, you also construct two types of pieced triangle units that become the set-in side pieces of the quilt top. The borders have cornerstones, which can be eliminated if you wish. Cut the border strips 1"–2" longer than the pattern states if you are removing the cornerstones.

Puss-in-the-Corner block
Block A
Finished size: 1"

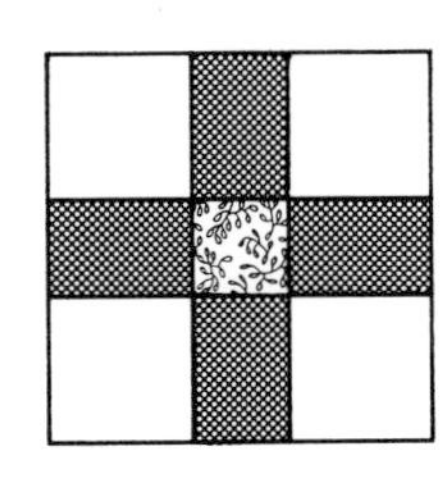

Cross block
Block B
Finished size: 1"

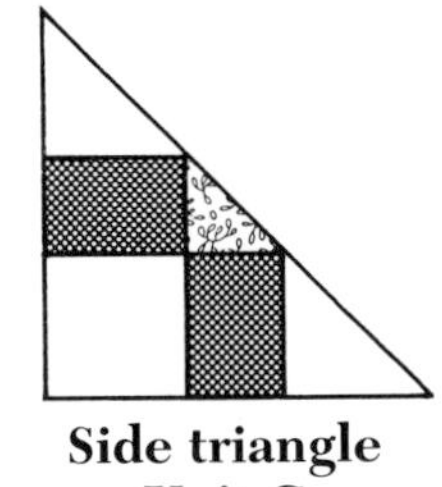

Side triangle
Unit C
Finished short sides: 1"

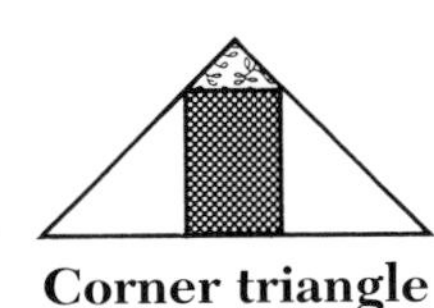

Corner triangle
Unit D
Finished long side: 1"

Cutting Instructions

Fabric #1: Red print, 10" x 15" piece
Cut:
- 2 strips, ¾" x 9" (Strata I)
- 2 strips, ⅞" x 9" (Strata II)
- 2 strips, ¾" x 6" (Strata V)
- 2 strips, ¾" x 8", cut into ⅞" segments (16 for Units C and D)
- 4 squares, ¾" x ¾" (cornerstones for inner border)
- 4 strips, 1½" x 7½" (outer border)

Fabric #2: Blue print, 11" x 13" piece
Cut:
- 6 strips, ¾" x 9" (Strata III)
- 2 strips, 1" x 9" (Strata IV)
- 4 strips, ¾" x 6½" (inner border)
- 4 squares, 1½" x 1½" (cornerstones for outer border)
- 4 squares, 1" x 1" (cornerstones for middle border)

Fabric #3: Tan print, 10" x 15" piece
Cut:
- 4 strips, ¾" x 9" (Strata IV)
- 3 strips, 1" x 9" (Strata III)
- 1 strip, ¾" x 9" (Strata II)
- 3 squares, 1¾" x 1¾" (oversized Unit C triangles)
- 2 squares, 1¼" x 1¼" (oversized Unit D triangles)
- 4 strips, 1" x 7" (middle border)

Fabric #4: Muslin, 11" x 11" piece
Cut:
- 4 strips, ⅞" x 9" (Strata I)
- 8 squares, 2" x 2" (oversized Units C and D triangles)
- 2 strips, ⅞" x 6" (Strata V)

Backing and Binding: 11" square, your fabric choice. To mimic model, use Fabric #1 and a rolled binding.

Assembly Instructions

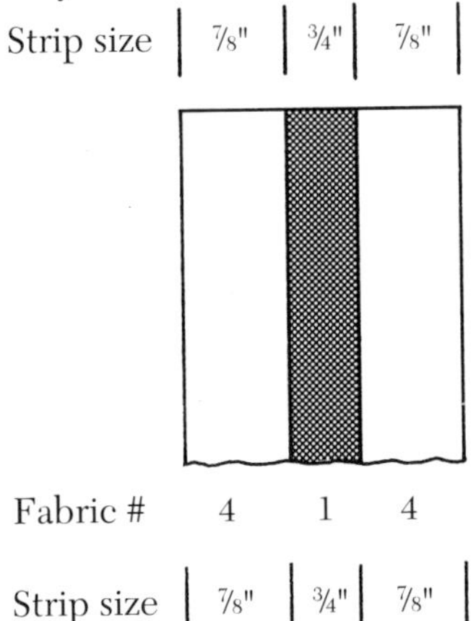

Strata I
2 sets
9" long

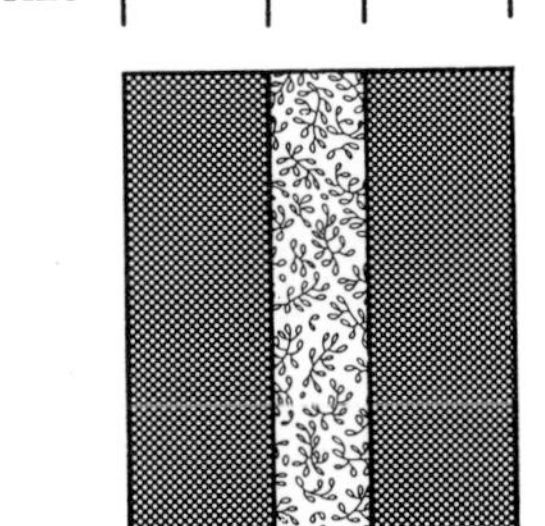

Strata II
1 set
9" long

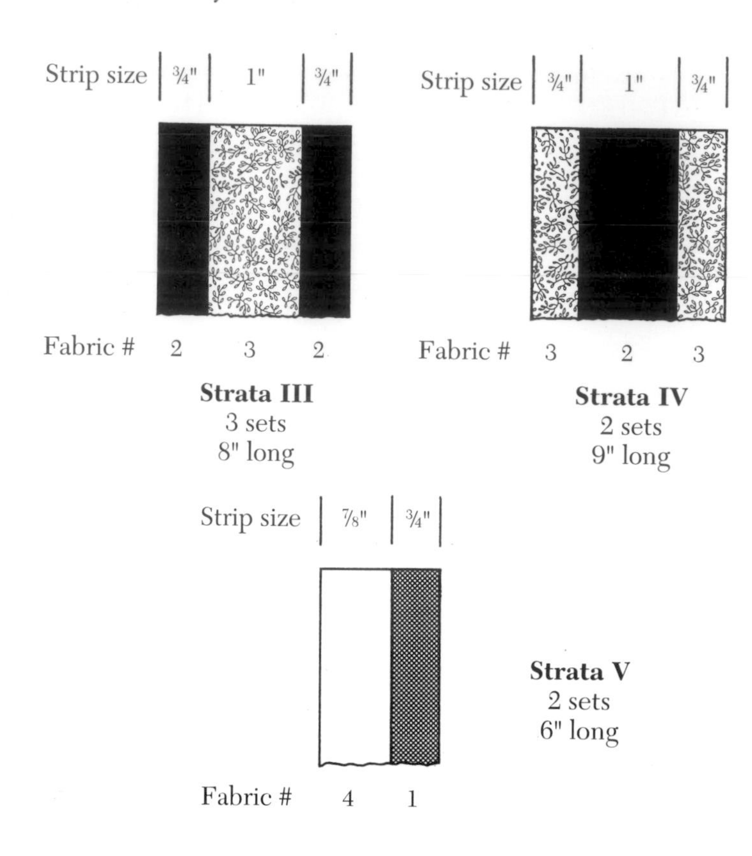

1. Assemble Strata I–V according to the diagrams. Make the number of sets as follows. Press all seams toward the dark strips.

Strata I:	Make 2
Strata II:	Make 1
Strata III:	Make 3
Strata IV:	Make 2
Strata V:	Make 2

2. Cut strata into segments as follows:

Strata I (⅞"):	18
Strata II (¾"):	9
Strata III (¾"):	32
Strata IV (1"):	16
Strata V (⅞"):	12

3. Assemble 16 Block A using the segments from Strata III and IV. Stack the segments in order on the work table and join them together as in the diagram. Press seams toward the center segment.

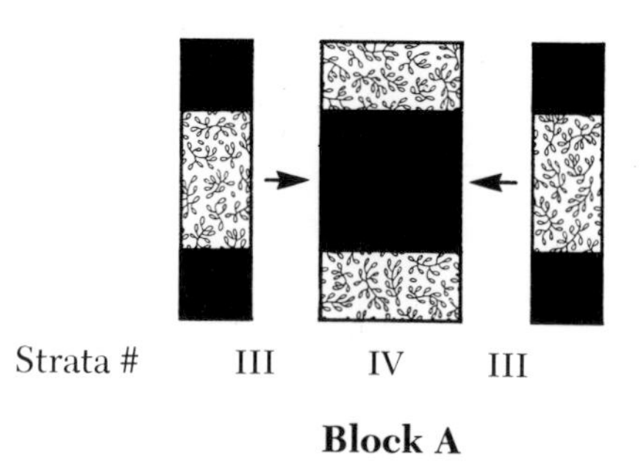

Block A

4. Assemble 9 Block B using the segments from Strata I and II. Stack the segments and join them together as in the diagram to form the blocks. Press seams toward the outer edges.

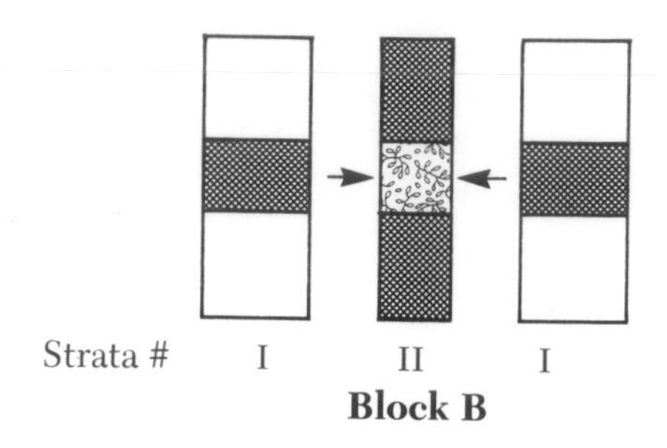

Block B

5. Cut the Fabric #3 squares, 1¾" x 1¾", into 12 quarter-square triangles. Cut the Fabric #4 squares, 2" x 2", into quarter-square triangles. Build Unit C, the set-in side triangle unit, with Strata V segments, the oversized Fabric #3 and #4 triangles, and the rectangles cut from Fabric #1. The first step is to join a Fabric #4 triangle to each long rectangle edge as in the diagram. Press the seam toward the triangle.

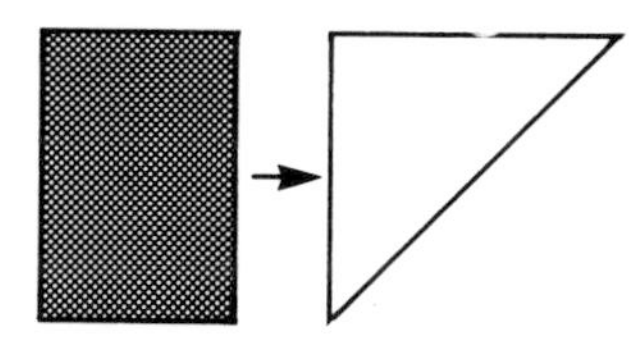

6. Join the Fabric #3 quarter-square triangles to the end of these units. Press the seam toward the rectangle.

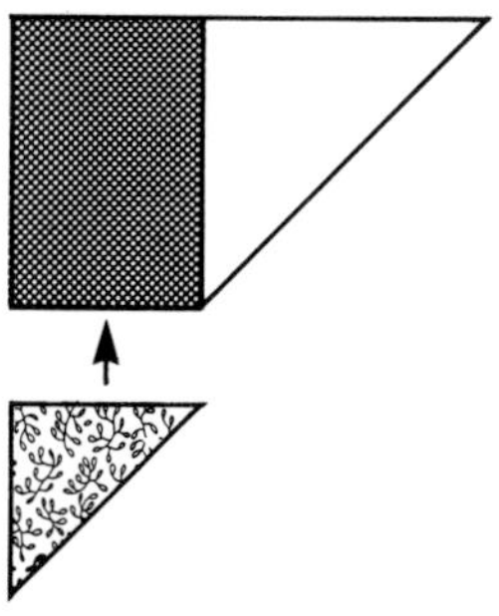

7. Add a segment from Strata V to the side of each unit created in Step 6. Press the seam toward the small triangle.

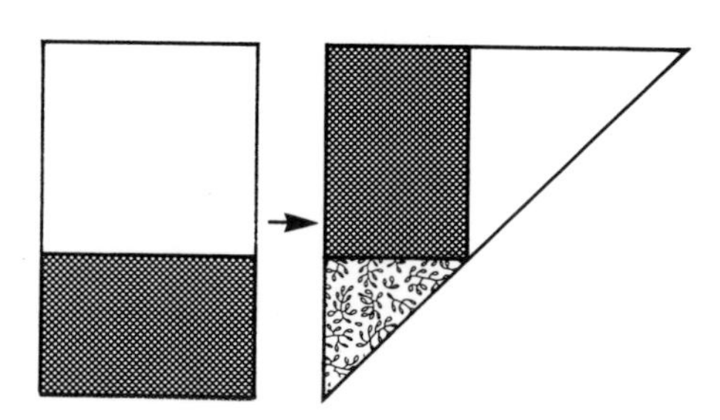

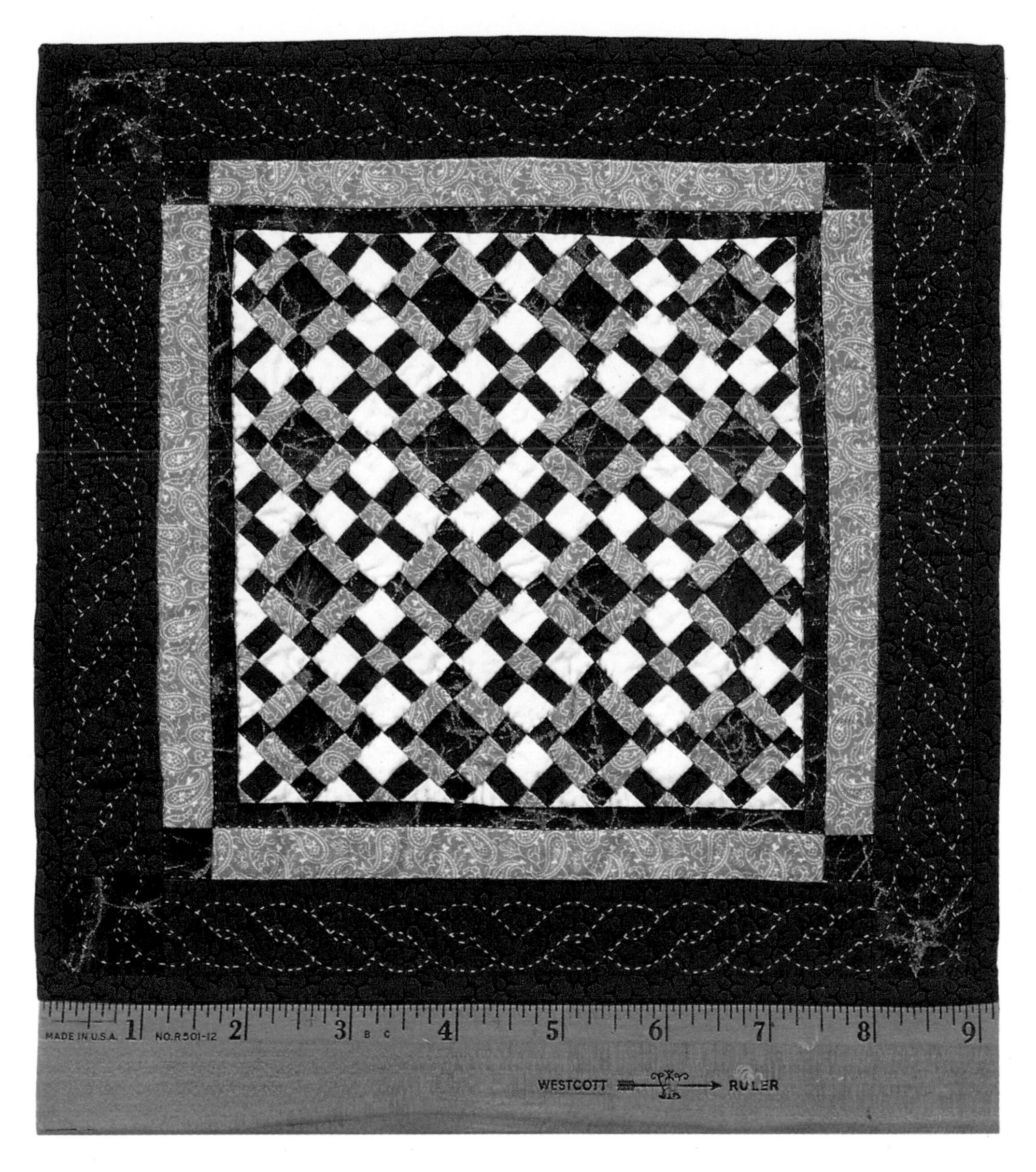

Cross-eyed Puss *by Donna Lynn Thomas, 1989, Frankfurt, West Germany, 9¾" x 9¾". This miniature quilt combines two different blocks, Cross and Puss-in-the-Corner, in a diagonal set to create an intricate design.*

8. Seam a large triangle to the end of each of these pieces to complete 12 Unit C. Press the seam toward the triangle.

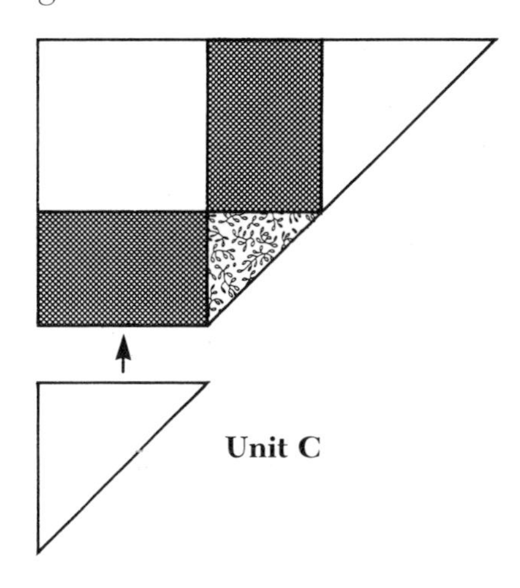

9. Cut the 1¼" Fabric #3 squares, into half-square triangles. Assemble 4 Unit D as shown in the diagram. Sew the last 8 Fabric #4 triangles to either side of the 4 remaining Fabric #1 rectangles. Press both seams toward the rectangle. Add a Fabric #3 half-square triangle to each of these pieces to complete Unit D. Press the last seam toward the small triangle.

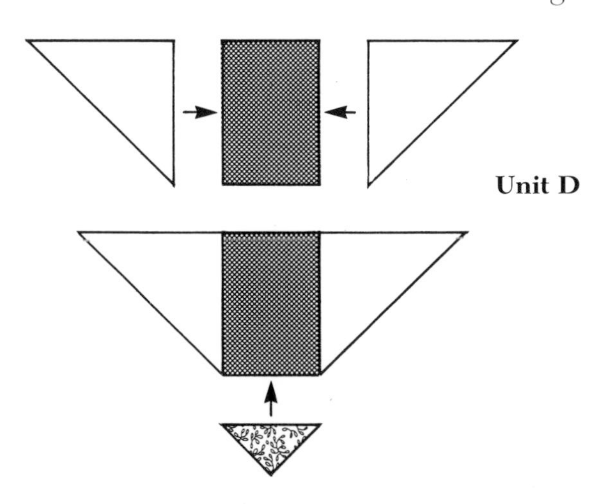

10. Assemble the blocks and side units into diagonal rows as in the Piecing Diagram and press the seams toward Block A. Join the rows to form the central body of the quilt top and press these seams in either direction.

Piecing Diagram

11. Trim the edges of the quilt to ¼" from the block points.
12. Measure and cut the Fabric #2 inner border strips to fit the quilt top through the center. Join a strip to two opposite sides of the quilt. Press the seams toward the strips. Add the cornerstones to both ends of the two remaining strips. Press the seams toward the strips. Sew these two strips to the top and bottom of the quilt.
13. Attach the middle and outer border strips in the same fashion.
14. Quilt and bind as desired.

Around the Twist

6" x 7 1/8"

This Around the Twist quilt, inspired by Trudie Hughes's creation in her book *Template-Free™ Quiltmaking*, uses two basic blocks to create an overall design. In this case, a Ninepatch variation is combined with three different Snowball blocks to produce an interlocking design. The finished size of the subunits is again 1/4", but the assembly is straightforward, making for a deceptively simple construction process. Please look carefully at the Piecing Diagram on page 44 to make sure the blocks are properly oriented in each row before joining. Have fun with this one—you'll be impressed with the results.

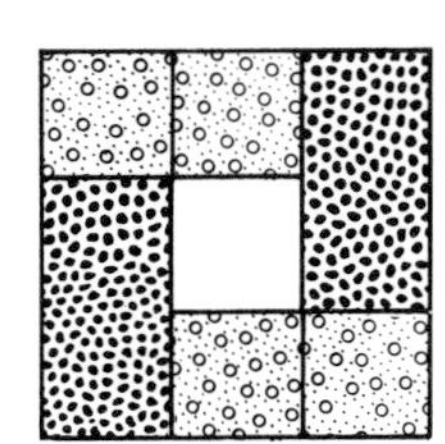

Twist block
Block A
Finished size: 3/4"

Cutting Instructions

Fabric #1: Blue print, 12" x 14" piece
Cut: 2 strips, 1" x 12" (Strata I)
16 squares, 1 1/8" x 1 1/8" (corners of Snowball blocks)
2 squares, 1 1/2" x 1 1/2" (corner triangles)
4 strips, 1 1/8" x 8" (border)

Fabric #2: Pink print, 7" x 14" piece
Cut: 4 strips, 3/4" x 12" (Strata I, II)
16 squares, 1 1/8" x 1 1/8" (corners of Snowball blocks)

Fabric #3: Tan print, 8" x 12" piece
Cut: 20 squares, 1 1/4" x 1 1/4" (Snowball blocks)
4 squares, 2 1/2" x 2 1/2" (side triangles)
1 strip, 3/4" x 12" (Strata I)

Backing and Binding: 10" square, your fabric choice. To mimic model, use Fabric #2 and a rolled binding.

Assembly Instructions

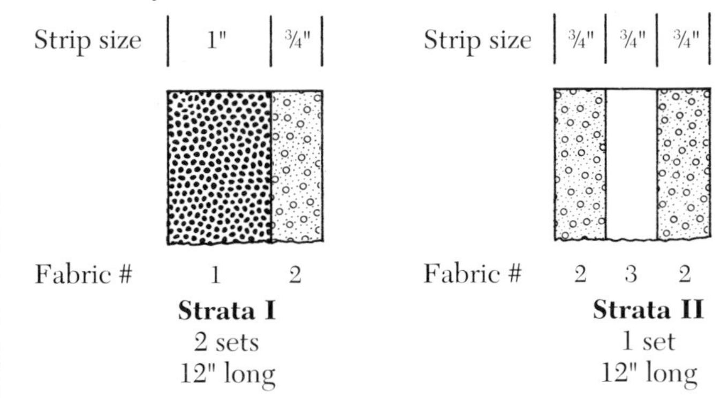

Strata I
2 sets
12" long

Strata II
1 set
12" long

1. Assemble 2 sets of Strata I and 1 set of Strata II as in the diagrams. Press the seams in Strata I toward Fabric #1. Press the seams in Strata II toward Fabric #2. Cut Strata I into 3/4" segments; you will need 24. Cut Strata II into 3/4" segments; you will need 12.
2. Using Strata I and II segments and following the diagram, assemble the Ninepatch Twist block (Block A). Press the seams to Strata I.

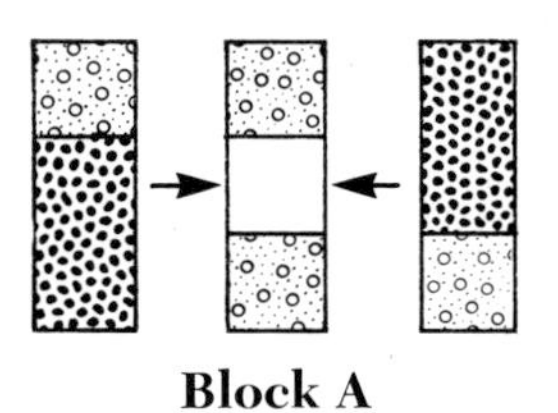

Block A

3. Make a stiff template of the Snowball Speedy and follow the instructions for cutting Snowball blocks on pages 31–32 to cut Snowballs in the following shapes.

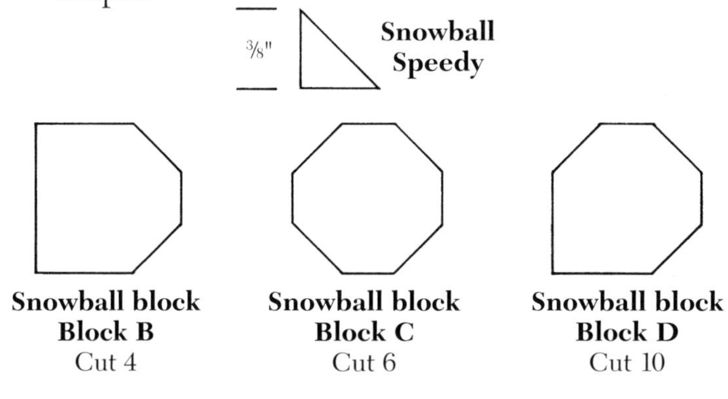

Snowball block
Block B
Cut 4

Snowball block
Block C
Cut 6

Snowball block
Block D
Cut 10

4. Cut each of the Fabric #1 and #2 squares, 1 1/8"x1 1/8", into 32 half-square triangles. Join 31 of each of the 2 sets of triangles to the corners of the different Snowball blocks as shown. Nub the triangle points as described in the instructions on page 32.

Block B: Make 2 blocks with Fabric #1 triangles
Make 2 blocks with Fabric #2 triangles

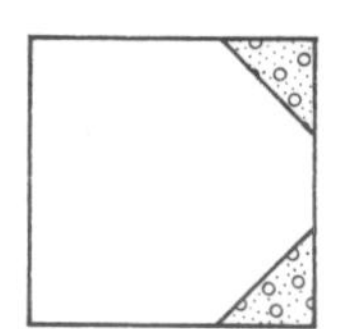
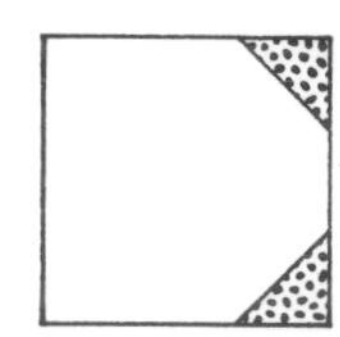

Block B
Assemble 2 of each color

Block C: Make 3 blocks with Fabric #1 triangles
Make 3 blocks with Fabric #2 triangles

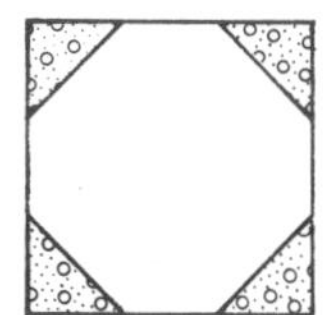
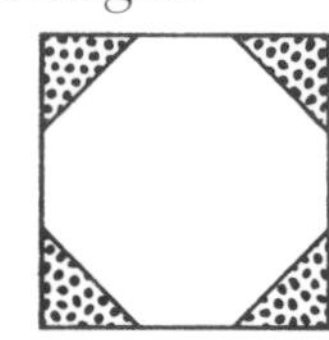

Block C
Assemble 3 of each color

Block D: Make 5 blocks with Fabric #1 triangles
Make 5 blocks with Fabric #2 triangles

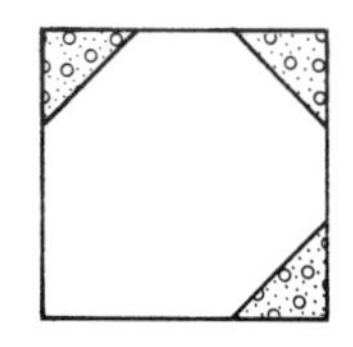
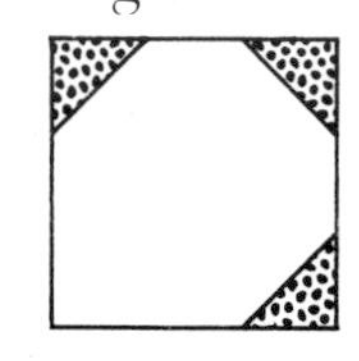

Block D
Assemble 5 of each color

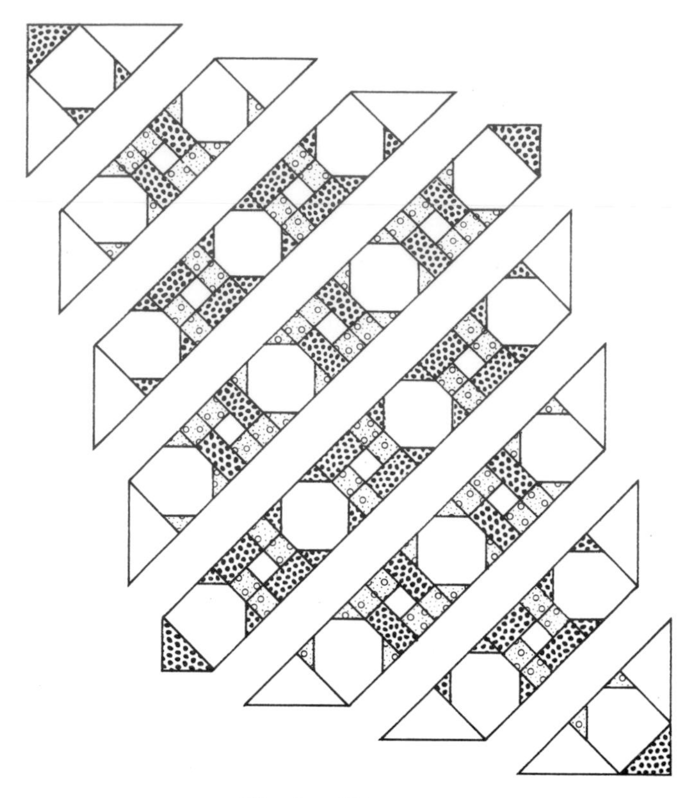

Piecing Diagram

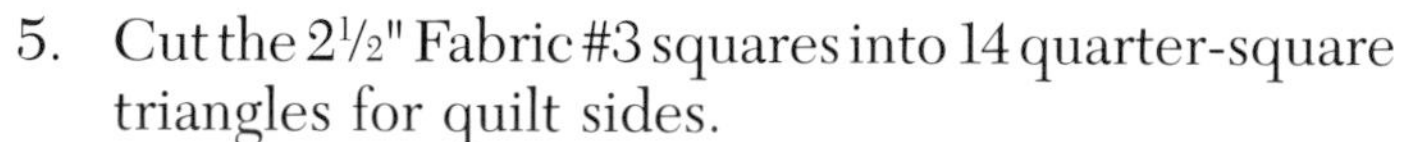

5. Cut the 2½" Fabric #3 squares into 14 quarter-square triangles for quilt sides.
6. Lay the blocks on the table and arrange them carefully according to the Piecing Diagram. You should be able to see the twist take shape. Lay the Fabric #3 side triangles at the ends of the rows and begin sewing the rows. The side triangles are oversized and will be trimmed after the rows are together. Press the seams toward the Ninepatch blocks and the side set triangles.
7. Join the rows together to form the quilt top. Press the seams in either direction. Cut the 1½" Fabric #1 squares into 4 half-square triangles and sew them to the corners of the quilt. Press the seams toward the outside edges. Trim the edges of the quilt ¼" from the block points.
8. Add the Fabric #1 borders, measuring the length and width of the quilt top through the center and cutting the border strips to these measurements.
9. Quilt and bind as desired.

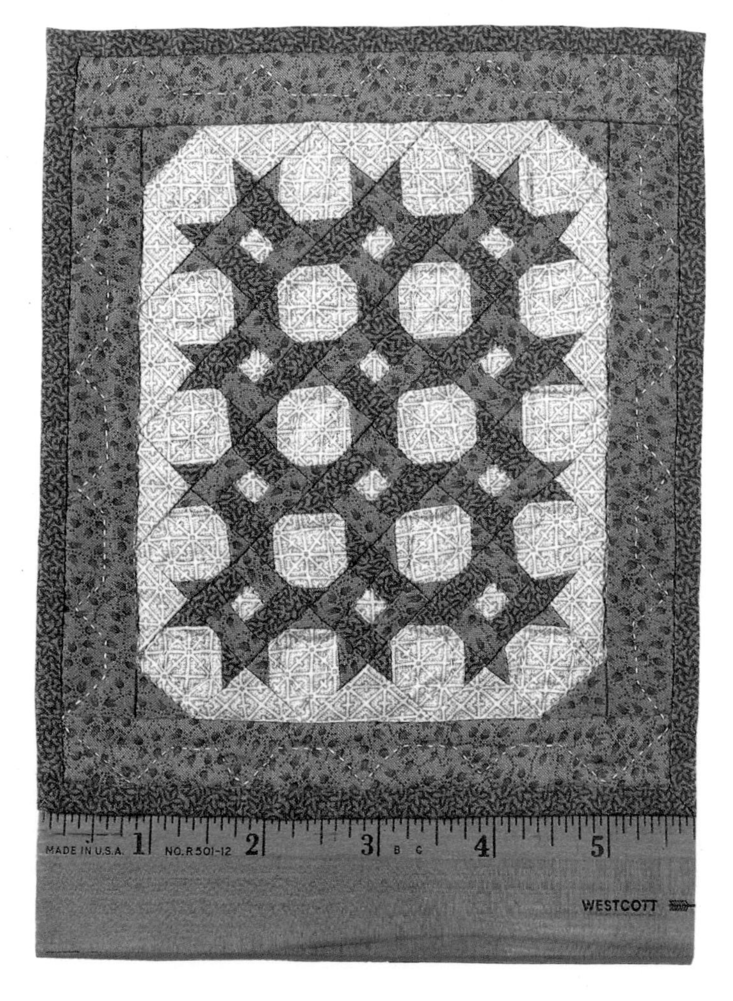

Around the Twist *by Donna Lynn Thomas, 1987, Brookhaven, Pennsylvania, 6" x 7⅛". The desire to recreate a quilt in Trudie Hughes's book* Template-Free™ Quiltmaking *resulted in this blue and rose treasure.*

Section II:

BIAS SQUARES

A bias square is a square composed of two right triangles joined together on the long side. This particular type of triangle combination is used extensively in both traditional and contemporary quilt patterns. Using traditional methods, two triangles are individually cut and then sewn together to form the bias square. With triangles as small as 1/4" finished size, the frustration of hand marking and sewing each tiny triangle would be enormous.

When I design miniatures, there are times when it is impossible to avoid dealing with tiny strips that can be as small as 1/8" in width when finished. The smaller the units become, the more difficult and frustrating it is to be accurate. Fortunately, there are many innovative quiltmakers who have developed timesaving and highly accurate methods to combat these problems. Some of these methods are the subject of discussion in this section.

Basic Concept

In most situations, the outside edges of a bias square should be cut on the straight of grain (S-O-G) to avoid stretching. This means that the seam running across the diagonal of the square is on the bias.

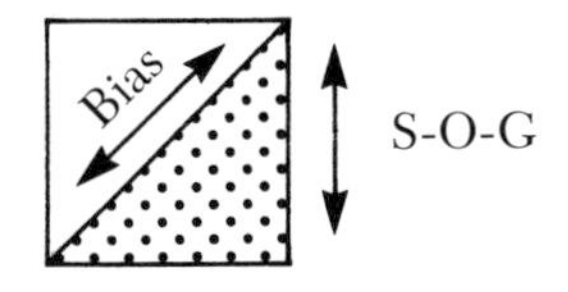

If two strips of fabric of appropriate width are sewn together as in S-O-G strata construction, squares may be cut from these strips on point to yield presewn bias squares.

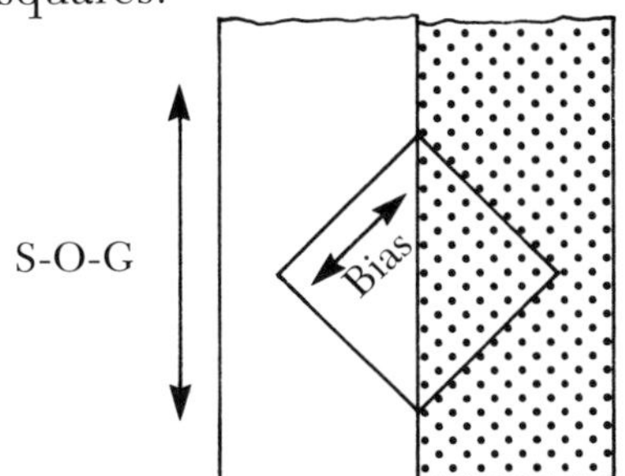

Strips cut on straight of grain. Cut squares have edges on bias.

If the strips are cut on the S-O-G as in a normal strata, then the resulting squares have the bias on the four outer edges and the S-O-G on the diagonal seam. This is not desirable. But, suppose the strips are cut on the bias. The resulting squares would then have outer edges on the S-O-G.

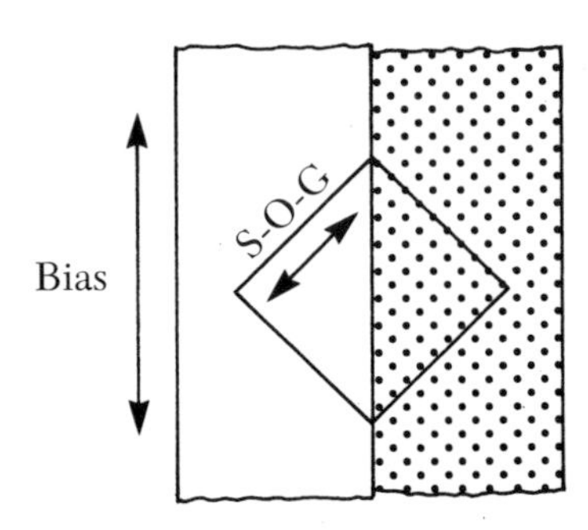

Strips cut on bias grain. Cut squares have edges on straight of grain.

This basic idea is the key to the bias square system. Bias strips are cut and sewn together. Bias squares are then diagonally cut from the bias strata. There are several things you need to know, though, before proceeding. For instance:

1. How do you cut bias strips?
2. What size strips do you cut?
3. How do you cut squares from the bias strata?

The following sections will help answer these and other questions.

Cutting Bias Strips

If the diagonal of any square cut on the S-O-G is on the bias, then strips cut from the diagonal of a square will have bias edges. Begin by making a center diagonal cut through a fabric square. Using the long center edge as the cutting guide, you can then cut strips from each large triangle.

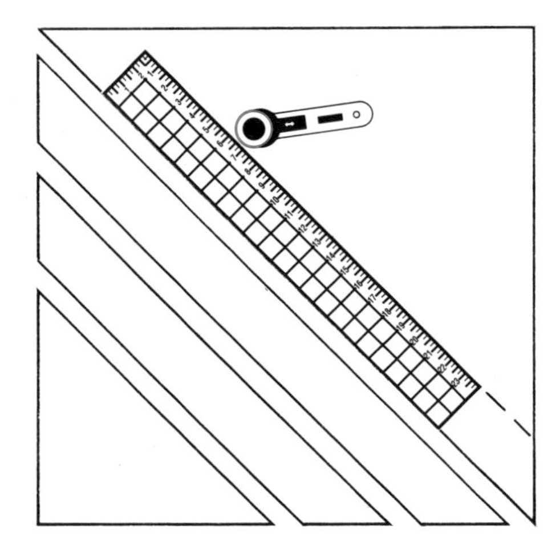

In fact, a complete square is unnecessary as long as one corner and its two edges are cut at a right angle. Measure an equal distance (x) along each right-angle side and make a mark. Make the first diagonal cut from point to point and proceed as with a regular square.

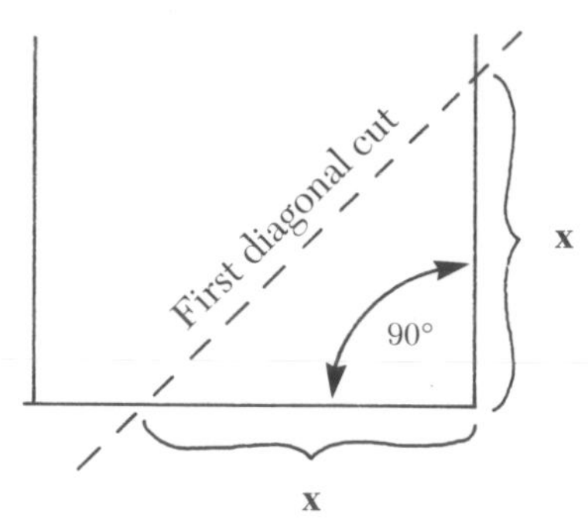

Another time-saver is to cut the strips for the two fabrics that will be sewn together for the bias squares at the same time. Steam the two fabrics right sides together (they adhere slightly when steamed), cut the square or right-angle sides, and begin cutting the diagonal strips. Not only are the strips cut at the same time, but they are also ready to be sewn together with their right sides facing.

Sewing Bias Strata

Bias strips are sewn with a ¼" seam along their longest edges. Press seams to the darker fabric unless there is a specific need for them to be pressed otherwise. They may be sewn in simple pairs or with several strips across. Normally, with miniatures, I cut my strips from squares of paired fabrics. As a result, there are two same-size strips of each color. I join these strips into pairs and then join the pairs to form a four-strip multiple bias strata.

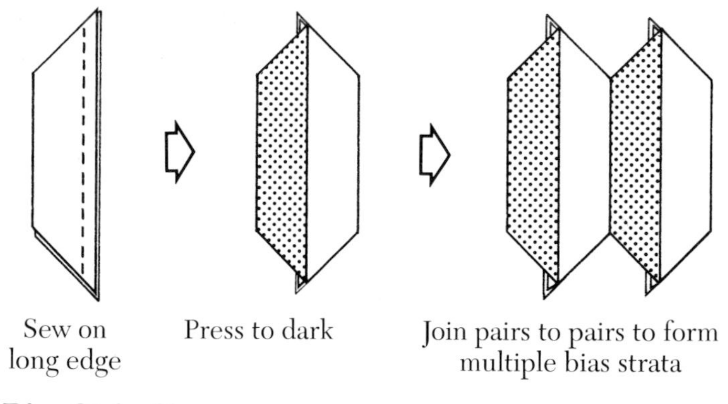

Bias Strip Size

Bias strips are cut a different width, depending on whether you are sewing simple pairs or multiple bias strata. When only two bias strips will be sewn together, cut the strips the width of the unfinished bias square. For instance, if you are cutting a 1" unfinished bias square (½" finished), then cut the bias strips 1" wide.

When sewing multiple strips, cut the bias strips ¼" wider than the unfinished bias square to account for the extra seam. For instance, to cut a 1" unfinished bias square, cut bias strips 1¼" wide (1" + ¼" = 1¼"). As a rule, I cut all my bias strips ¼" larger than the cut bias square so that the resulting waste triangles are larger.

Cutting Bias Squares

Once the bias strips are cut and sewn together, bias squares may be cut from the bias strata. Cut a square, see-through plastic template with ¼" seam allowances included. Draw a diagonal line on the template bisecting the square. Tape the template onto the corner of a hard plastic ruler. You are now ready to rotary cut squares right from the fabric.

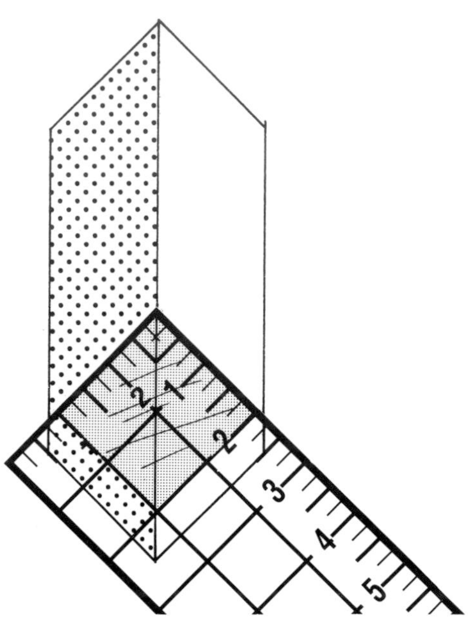

Easier still is the use of the Bias Square®, a 6" square ruler with ⅛" marks on the side. A diagonal line bisecting the ruler makes it easy to establish your cutting line.

Using the same hypothetical 1" bias square mentioned before, begin with the lower end of the bias strata and put the Bias Square or template over the strips with the 1" markings just inside the lower raw edges. Cut the top two edges of the square from raw edge to raw edge. Set the resulting square aside and continue to cut as many bias squares from the strata as possible, being sure that the 1" square markings are always within the strata boundaries and not extending past the lower point.

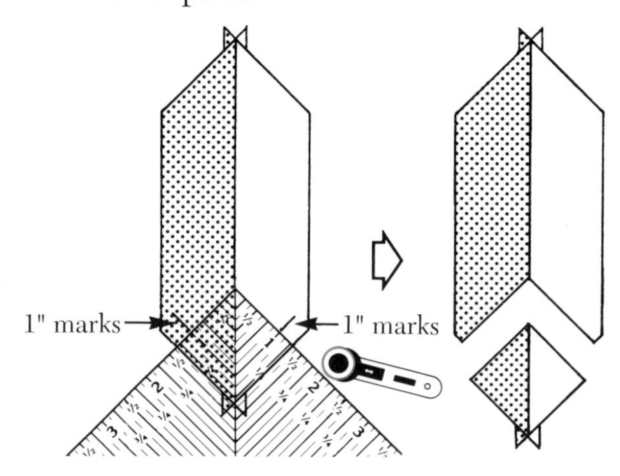

Now, go back to each cut piece, turn the lower two edges of each bias square up, and trim them to size with the Bias Square®.

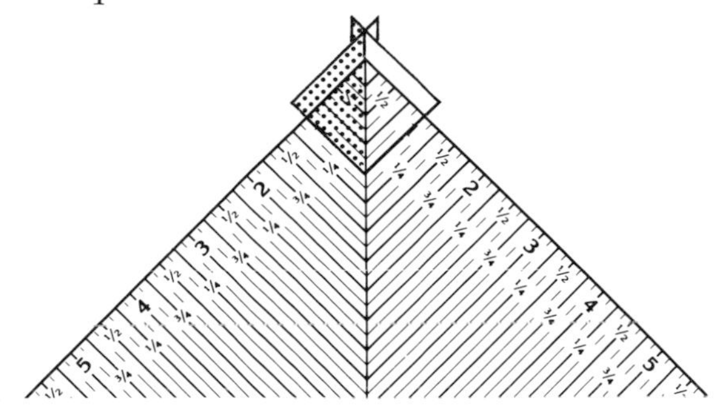

When cutting bias squares from multiple bias strata, use the same procedure, being careful to always cut from the lowest points across the bias strata before cutting farther up the strata. Move systematically from either left to right or right to left, cutting all the low points first.

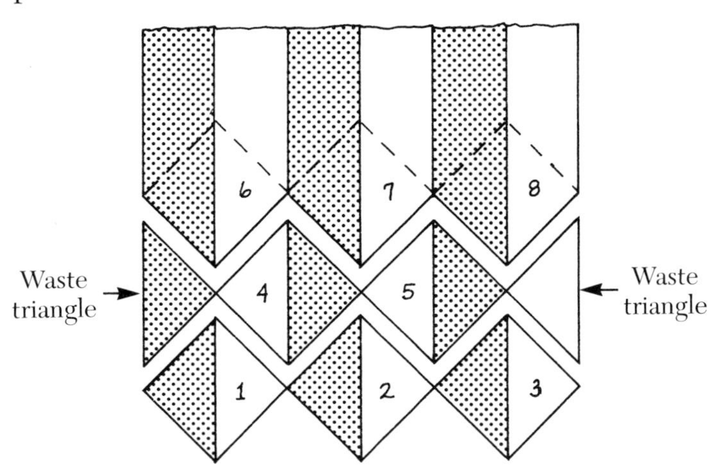

Cut from lowest point across the strata. Waste triangles are produced along the edges of the bias strata.

As you cut bias squares from bias strata, you will notice that there are leftover waste triangles from the edges of the strips. You will also notice that fewer waste triangles are produced when you cut from multiple bias strata than from simple bias strata. If large enough, these single waste triangles can be used in many patterns that call for singly cut triangles.

If you have a liking for scrap quilts, save those waste triangles in a plastic bag for future use. As I mentioned earlier, I always cut my bias strips ¼" larger than the cut bias square even if not making multistrips. This is so that the waste triangles are always large enough for another project. An oversized triangle is preferable with miniatures, anyway; it can be cut back to size later. A too-small waste triangle is truly wasted.

The following is a yield chart for bias-square production. It lists the approximate number of bias squares of a particular size that may be cut from a number of different-size fabric squares. The figures are based on single bias strata with strips cut the width of the cut bias square. More bias squares can be produced by switching to multiple bias strata.

Bias Square Yield Chart

Bias Square Size	**Bias Square Yield from Fabric Squares**						
	3"	4"	5"	6"	7"	8"	9"
¼" (¾" cut)	10	16	28	42	56	74	96
⅜" (⅞" cut)	8	14	22	30	42	56	72
½" (1" cut)	6	10	16	24	34	44	54
¾" (1¼" cut)	4	6	10	16	22	30	36

Note: These figures are based on single bias strata that are composed of bias strips cut the width of the unfinished bias square. The yield will change if the bias strips are cut ¼" wider and multiple bias strata are sewn. Use these figures as guides and always estimate on the side of excess to allow for errors.

Seam and Cut

The seam-and-cut concept is based on the idea of sewing first and cutting to size later. I ran across this idea in Mary Hickey's book *Little By Little*. Although the basic premise has been used in various aspects of quiltmaking, Mary took the idea and applied it in a creative way.

Primarily, the idea has been used for strata and bias-strip construction where seams are sewn first and shapes cut second. The idea of setting oversized triangles on the sides of diagonally set quilt tops that are later cut to size is based on the same premise. A high degree of accuracy can be achieved by cutting after the seam is sewn.

Taken a bit further, the idea can be successfully applied to problem areas in miniature construction. For example, in many instances, a ⅛" wide sashing is necessary to keep the quilt to scale. It can be difficult, though, to attach a ⅝" cut strip to a heavily pieced miniature block or quilt row. Often, slight shifting occurs in the sashing along the seam as the presser foot moves over it.

The solution is to cut a sashing that is ¼" wider than needed, seam it on, and then trim it to the desired finished size plus ¼". There may still be some shifting when the other side of the sashing is sewn, but half the problem has been eliminated. When trimming the pieces back, it is important to cut very slowly and accurately. The seam-and-cut technique is helpful in places where thick layers or seams do not allow the ruler to lie flat against the rotary mat. Unless you firmly press the ruler and underlying layers flat while cutting, you will not be able to properly guide the rotary cutter, and the result will be a wobbly cut. The pattern for the Autumn Leaves quilt employs the seam-and-cut technique in attaching its 1/8" sashings.

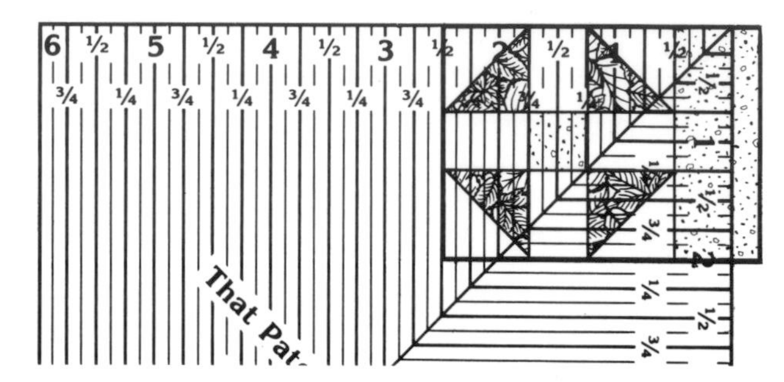

After sewing it to the block, trim sashing to desired finished size plus 1/4"

Another pattern using the seam-and-cut idea is Moonlight Regatta (page 60). The application is slightly different but provides the perfect opportunity to adapt the concept. The sailboats have tiny 1/8" masts. Rather than cut 5/8" segments for the masts or incorporate strips of that size in a strata, it is easier to cut one very wide piece, seam it onto one sail, and cut it back to size (1/8" + remaining 1/4" seam allowance = 3/8"). The remainder of the wide piece can then be sewn to the second sail, cut to fit, and so on, until all the sails have their masts. Instead of crooked masts, it becomes a breeze (so to speak!) to create perfectly straight narrow masts.

These are the only two patterns that have built-in seam-and-cut instructions, although there are many instances where you may opt to do so yourself. An example would be the 5/8" wide black strip in Strata II of Little St. Nick. It could easily be cut 1/4" wider, sewn in place, and trimmed to 3/8" before building on the rest of the strata. It's a good idea to train yourself to see the potential use of the seam-and-cut concept and adapt it to different situations.

The following patterns all make use of bias squares in some shape or form. As in Section I, they are arranged in order of difficulty. Please remember that each section builds on and assumes mastery of the skills from the preceding sections. Begin with the warm-up project and make as many warm-up samples as needed to become comfortable with the skills. Be sure to check each seam for accuracy before trimming it.

Warm-Up Project: Shoo-Fly

8¼" x 10½"

Bias-square construction and simple strip piecing are all that are needed to make the traditional Shoo-Fly pattern. The sashings between the blocks are ¼" wide and suitable for the seam-and-cut method. Normally, it's not necessary to use the seam-and-cut method on ¼" sashings, but it never hurts to practice.

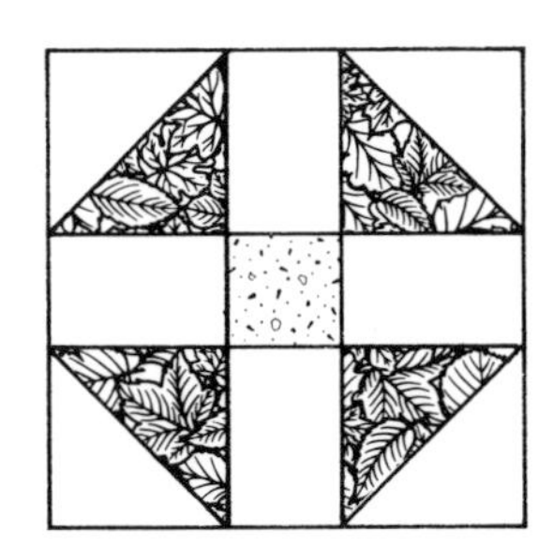

Shoo-Fly block
Finished size: 2"

Cutting Requirements

Fabric #1: Green print, 10" x 15" piece
Cut: 1 square, 8" x 8" (bias squares)
4 strips, 2" x 9" (border)

Fabric #2: Peach print, 8" x 11" piece
Cut: 1 strip, 1" x 8" (Strata I)
6 strips, 1" x 10" (sashings)

Fabric #3: Tan print, 10" square
Cut: 1 square, 8" x 8" (bias squares)
2 strips, 1¼" x 8" (Strata I)
2 strips, 1" x 8" (subcut into 12 rectangles, 1" x 1¼")

Backing and Binding: 10" x 13" piece, your fabric choice. To mimic model, use Fabric #1 and a rolled binding (see page 84).

Assembly Instructions

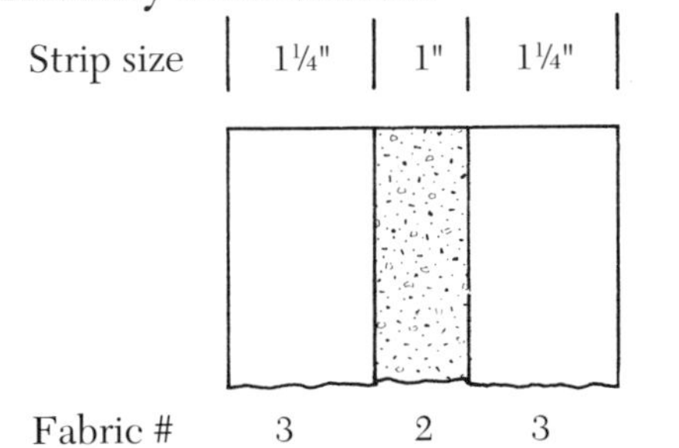

Strata I
8" long

1. Assemble Strata I according to the diagram. Cut strata into 1" segments; you will need 6.
2. Steam the two 8" fabric squares from Fabrics #1 and #3 together, right sides facing. Cut them in half on the diagonal and cut 1¼" bias strips from the diagonal edges.
3. Seam the pairs of strips together on their long edges and carefully press the seams toward the darker fabric.
4. Cut 1¼" bias squares from the bias strata; you will need 24.
5. Lay out the bias squares, strata segments, and Fabric #3 rectangles, 1" x 1¼", as they will be assembled. Join a bias square to either side of the rectangles as in the diagram. Press seams toward the rectangles.

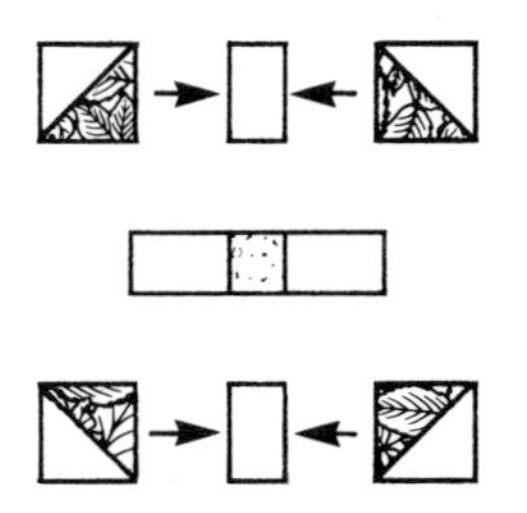

6. Join the bias square rows you just completed to each side of a strata segment to complete the 6 Shoo-Fly blocks. Press the seams toward the center. Lay them on the table with 2 across and 3 down as in the photo.
7. Cut 3 strips, 2½" long, from the 1" x 10" Fabric #2 sashing strips. These are the short center sashings. Join them to the right sides of the 3 blocks on the left. Press the seams toward the sashings.

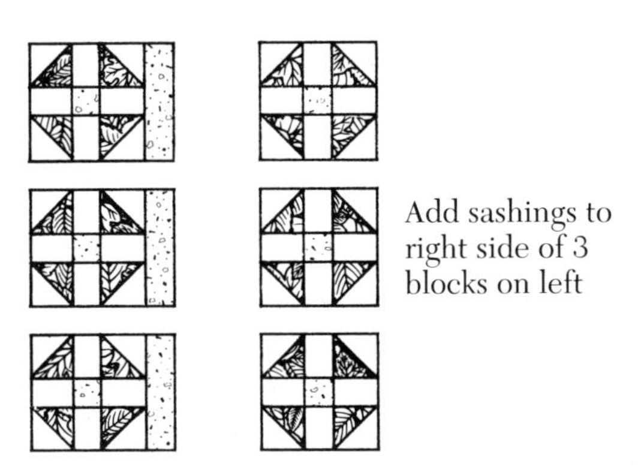

Add sashings to right side of 3 blocks on left

8. Cut sashing strips back to ½" wide. Be sure to press the layers flat with a ruler to get an accurate cut.

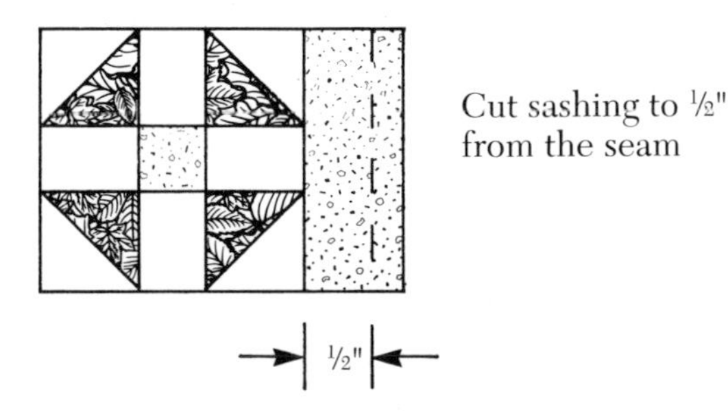

Cut sashing to ½" from the seam

9. Join the remaining 3 blocks to the other side of the 3 short center sashing strips to complete the rows. Press the seams toward the sashings.
10. Cut 2 strips, 4¾" long, from the 1" Fabric #2 sashing strips. These are the inner horizontal sashings. Join them to the lower edge of the top and middle rows. Cut them back to ½". Press the seams toward the sashings.

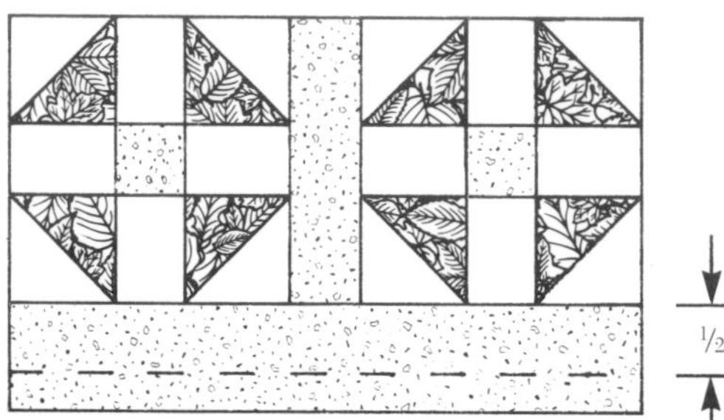

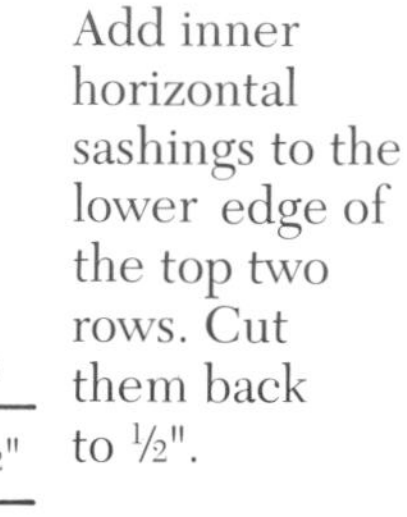

Add inner horizontal sashings to the lower edge of the top two rows. Cut them back to ½".

11. On the wrong side, make extension marks on the horizontal sashings where the inner sashing seams lie. These will be the guidelines to align the short sashes when joining the rows together (see page 22).
12. Join the rows together, aligning the sashing seams on one row with the guide marks on the sashing of the adjoining row. Press seams toward sashings.
13. Cut 2 sashing strips the length of the center body of the quilt. Attach them to the sides of your quilt and trim them back to ½".
14. Cut 2 sashing strips the width of the center body of the quilt including the side sashings. Attach them to the top and bottom of the quilt and trim to ½" wide.
15. Following the directions for straight-sewn borders on page 23, attach the Fabric #1 border strips.
16. Quilt and bind as desired.

Shoo-Fly *by Donna Lynn Thomas, 1990, Frankfurt, West Germany, 8¼" x 10½". Shoo-Fly is a simple pattern that becomes elegant in peach and green. Quilted by Ann Marie Eberlin.*

Churn Dash

8½" x 11½"

This quilt has a fancy border. If you do not wish to add the outer border, you can substitute a ½" Fabric #1 border instead. Remember that only 32 bias squares are needed if the outer border is eliminated.

Churn Dash is another traditional pattern that is only slightly more complicated than the Shoo-Fly warm up. In fact, the finished size of these bias squares is ½" instead of the usual ⅜" or ¼". Enjoy!

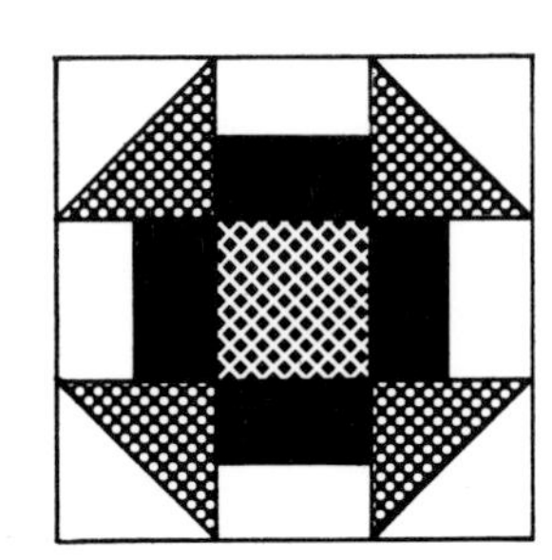

Churn Dash block
Finished size: 1½"

Cutting Requirements

Fabric #1: Red print, 12" x 22" piece
Cut: 2 squares, 10" x 10" (bias squares)
4 squares, 1" x 1" (outer border)

Fabric #2: Green print, 8" x 13" piece
Cut: 3 strips, ¾" x 12" (strata)
4 strips, 1" x 10" (inner border)

Fabric #3: Light print, 18" x 22" piece
Cut: 2 squares, 10" x 10" (bias squares)
3 strips, ¾" x 12" (strata)
7 squares, 2" x 2" (alternate plain blocks)
4 strips, 1½" x 10" (middle border)

Fabric #4: Red plaid, 3" x 5" piece
Cut: 8 squares, 1" x 1" (Churn Dash centers)

Backing and Binding: 13" square, your choice of fabric. To mimic model, use Fabric #2 and a rolled binding.

Assembly Instructions

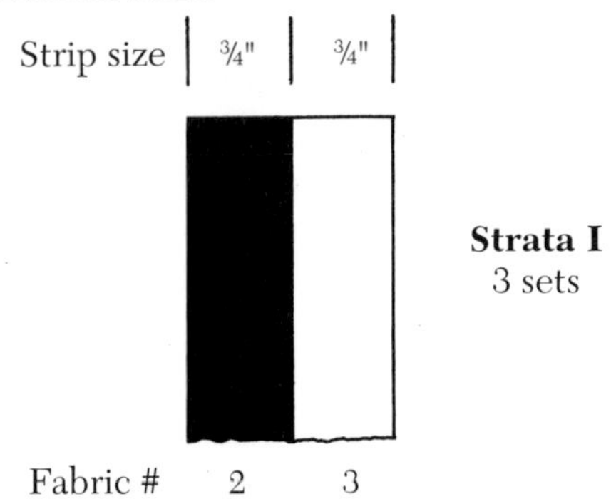

Strata I
3 sets

1. Assemble 3 sets of the strata units as in the diagram. Press seams toward Fabric #3. Cut strata into 1" segments; you will need 32.
2. Steam the 10" Fabric #1 and Fabric #3 squares right sides together. Cut 1¼" bias strips and seam them into pairs. Press half of the seams toward the light and half toward the dark. Join the like pairs to form multiple bias strata and cut 1" bias squares as described below.
   a. Cut 38 bias squares with seams toward the dark and reserve them for the outer border.
   b. Cut 34 bias squares with seams toward the light and reserve them for the outer border.
   c. Cut 32 bias squares for the 8 Churn Dash blocks with either seam direction, although it's a good idea if the bias squares in each block are alike.
3. Lay the different components for the Churn Dash block in order on the work table: bias squares, strata segments, and plain 1" Fabric #4 squares. Assemble the rows as indicated in the diagram. Press the seams toward the strata units.

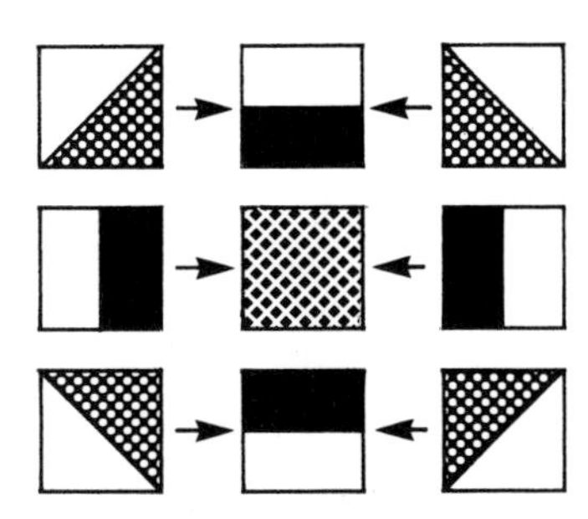

4. Join the rows together to form the Churn Dash blocks. Press the seams toward the outside edges.

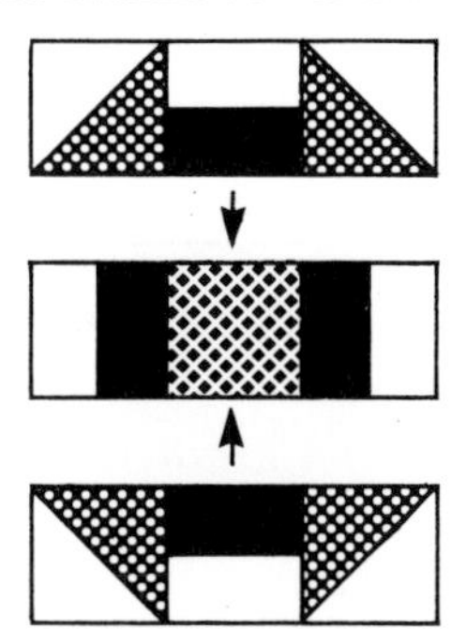

5. Lay the Churn Dash blocks on the table alternately with the plain blocks as in the photo. Assemble the blocks into rows. Press the seams toward the plain blocks. Join the rows to form the center of the quilt. Press the seams in either direction.
6. Following the directions for straight-set borders on page 23, attach the Fabric #2 inner border strips.
7. Attach the Fabric #3 middle border strips in the same fashion.
8. From the 72 reserved border bias squares, assemble 32 bias-square pairs as in the diagram. When joining bias squares to form pairs, use 2 bias squares with seams pressed in opposite directions for easy assembly. You can match and butt the diagonal seams if they are pressed in opposite directions. Press seams in the direction indicated in the diagram.

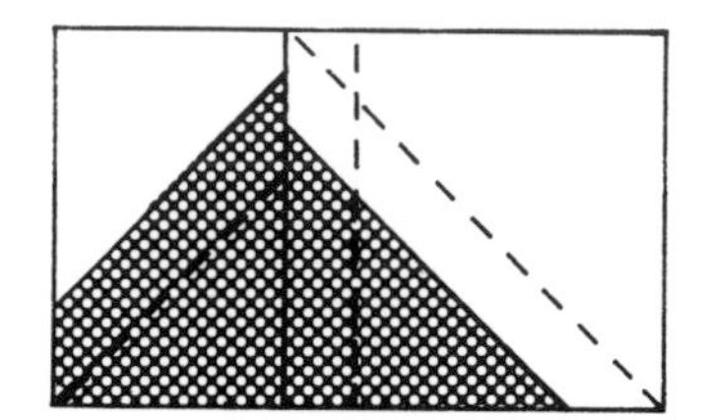

9. Assemble the side borders using photo as a guide. Press seams as shown in step 8 to eliminate bulk.
10. Align the plain square in the middle of the border strip with the center row of the middle Churn Dash block and pin in place. Next, pin the outer corners and adjust the border to fit the quilt top edge. Pin the center, if necessary. Sew the borders to the quilt top. Press seams toward the center of the quilt.
11. Assemble the top and bottom borders as in the photo. Press seams in alternate directions to eliminate bulk. The seam joining the bias squares on each end of the border strips should be pressed toward the end of the border strips.
12. Align the plain square in the middle of each border strip with the middle of the alternate plain block in the quilt body. Sew the top and bottom borders onto the quilt and press the seams toward the center of the quilt.
13. Quilt and bind as desired.

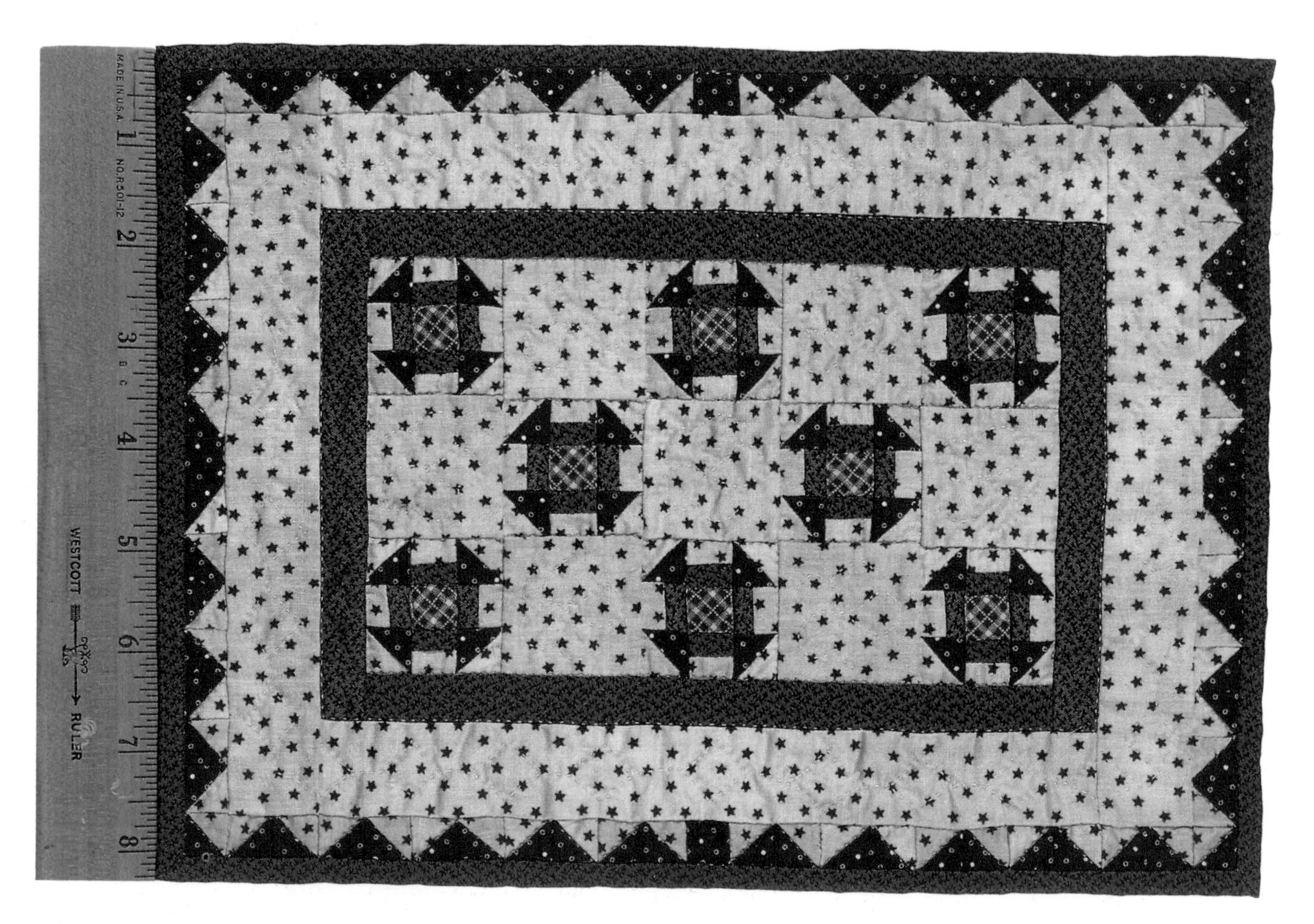

***Churn Dash** by Donna Lynn Thomas, 1989, Frankfurt, West Germany, 8½" x 11½". Reproduction antique fabrics are the perfect complement to an old pattern such as Churn Dash. The fancy border adds an exciting final touch.*

Cake Stand

9⅞" x 12"

The Cake Stand block is a relatively easy block to assemble. Be careful, though, when choosing fabrics for your quilt. If you make poor fabric choices, the Cake Stand points may disappear or the alternate plain blocks may overpower the pieced blocks. Refer to the Fabric Choices section on pages 6–9 for more information.

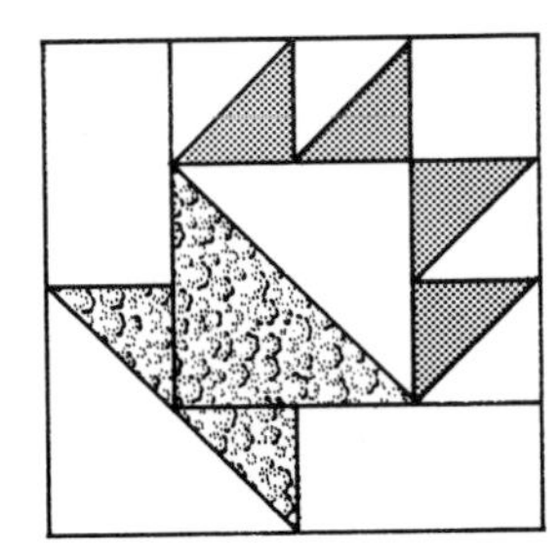

Cake Stand block
Finished size: 1½"

Cutting Requirements

Fabric #1: Green print, 10" x 14" piece
Cut: 1 square, 6" x 6" (large bias squares)
12 squares, 1¼" x 1¼" (base triangles)
4 strips, 1" x 9" (inner border)

Fabric #2: Medium pink print, 9" square
Cut: 1 square, 8" x 8" (small bias squares)

Fabric #3: Light pink, 14" x 18" piece
Cut: 1 square, 6" x 6" (large bias squares)
1 square, 8" x 8" (small bias squares)
24 rectangles, ⅞" x 1¼" (side strips)
6 squares, 1¾" x 1¾" (large triangles)
12 squares, ⅞" x ⅞" (small squares)

Fabric #4: Green paisley, 12" x 14" piece
Cut: 6 squares, 2" x 2" (alternate plain blocks)
4 strips, 2" x 12" (outer border)

Fabric #5: Pink plaid, 9" square
Cut: 3 squares, 3¾" x 3¾" (oversized side set triangles)
2 squares, 2" x 2" (corner triangles)

Backing and Binding: 13" x 15" piece, your fabric choice. To mimic model, use Fabric #4 and a rolled binding.

Assembly Instructions

1. Steam the 6" Fabric #1 and Fabric #3 squares right sides together and cut 1½" bias strips from them. Seam the strips into pairs and sew like-size pairs together. Press the seams toward the dark fabric. Cut 1¼" bias squares from the bias strata; you will need 12.
2. Steam the 8" Fabric #2 and Fabric #3 squares right sides together and cut 1⅛" bias strips from them. Seam the strips into pairs and sew like-size pairs together. Cut ⅞" bias squares from the strata; you will need 48.
3. Cut the 1¼" Fabric #1 squares in half on the diagonal to form 24 half-square triangles. Seam these onto the 24 Fabric #3 rectangles as in the diagram. Please note that 12 of the triangles face in one direction and the other 12 face in the opposite direction. Press the seams toward the dark.

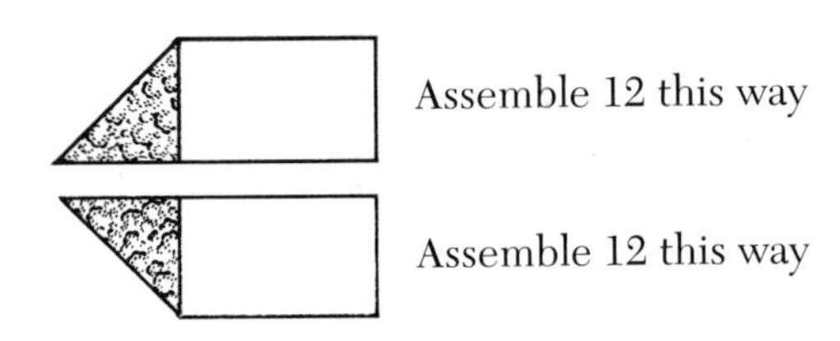

4. Cut the 1¾" Fabric #3 squares in half on the diagonal to form 12 half-square triangles.
5. Join the 48 small bias squares into pairs with 12 pairs going one direction and the other 12 pairs going the opposite direction. Press seams in the direction indicated in the diagram.

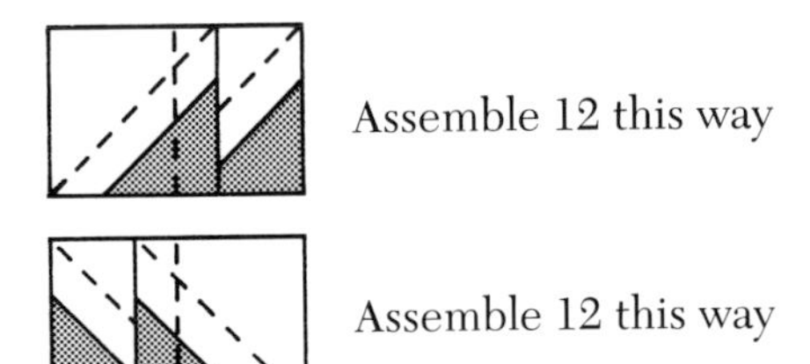

6. Lay the large bias squares, the small bias-square pairs, and the small Fabric #3 squares on the table as shown in the diagram.

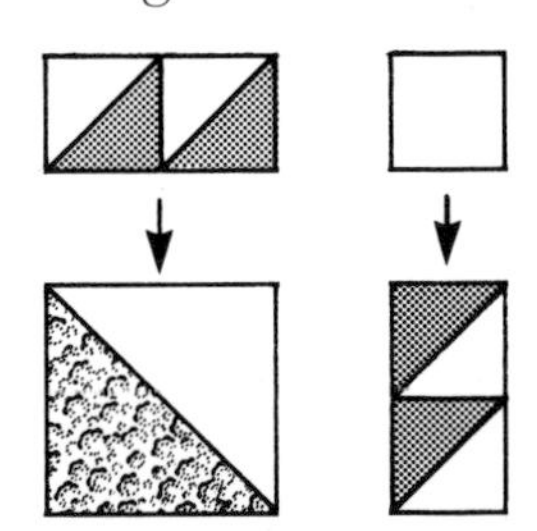

7. Seam the top bias-square pairs to the top of the large bias squares. Press the seams toward the large bias squares.

8. Join the small squares to the ends of the other bias-square pairs. Press the seams toward the plain squares.
9. Join these units to the right side of the large bias squares and bias-square pairs. Press the seams toward the large bias squares.

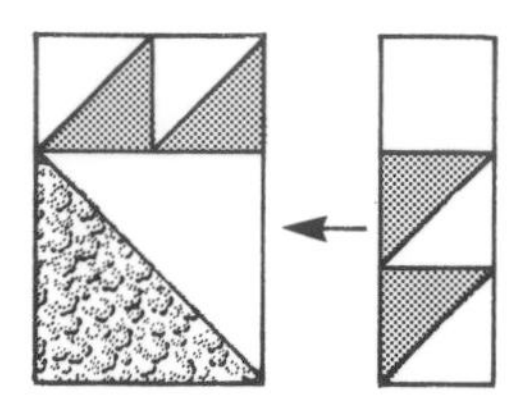

10. Join the rectangle/triangle units formed in step 3 to either side of the completed bias-square units. Press seams toward the rectangle units.

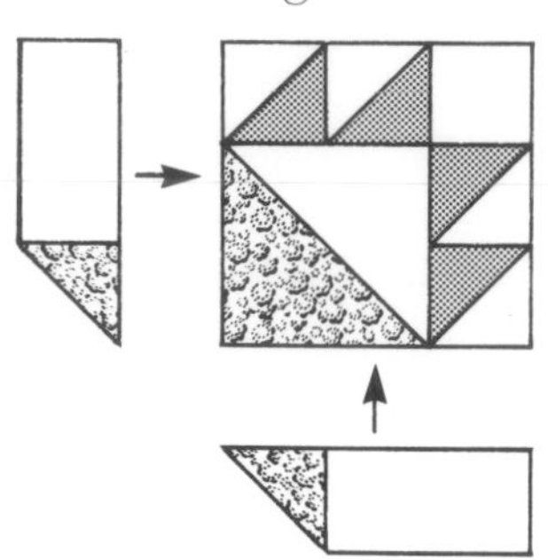

Cake Stand *by Donna Lynn Thomas, 1989, Frankfurt, West Germany, 9⅞" x 12". The paisley print brings this pretty quilt together for a soft look. Quilted by Ann Marie Eberlin.*

11. Sew the 12 Fabric #3 triangles formed in step 4 to the bottoms of the Cake Stand blocks. When laying the oversized triangle on the seam, center the point of the triangle with the upper point of the large bias square. Press the seams toward the Fabric #3 triangles. On the right side of the block, trim the oversized triangle to fit. Use the seam between the rectangle/triangle unit and the bias square as a guide for cutting it back to size.

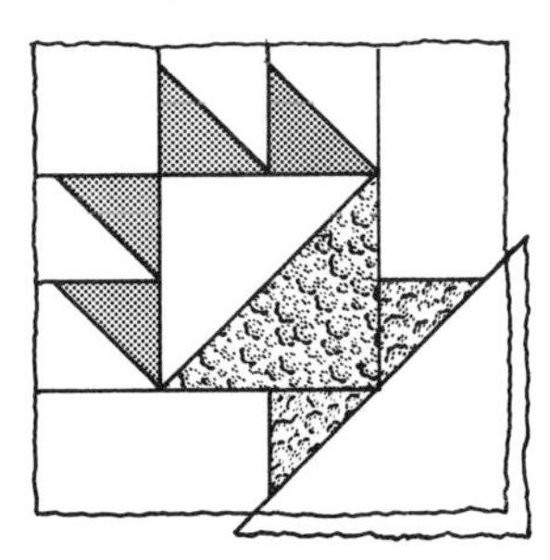

Trim excess from triangle

12. Cut the 3¾" Fabric #5 squares on both diagonals to form 10 quarter-square triangles.
13. Lay the Cake Stand blocks, 2" Fabric #4 plain blocks, and the Fabric #5 quarter-square triangles on the table in diagonal rows. Seam the units into rows as in the diagram. Press the seams toward the plain blocks and triangles.

Piecing Diagram

14. Join the rows to form the quilt top center. Press the seams in either direction.
15. Cut the 2" Fabric #5 squares in half to form the 4 quilt corner triangles. Sew onto the corners.
16. Using the outer corners of the Cake Stand blocks as a guide, cut the outer edges of the quilt center to ¼" from the guides. Use the horizontal and vertical ruler lines to cut the corners of the quilt square.
17. Cut two of the Fabric #1 inner border strips to fit the center length of the quilt. Seam to either side of the quilt. Press the seams out.
18. Cut the remaining inner border strips to fit the center width and seam them to the top and bottom of the quilt. Press the seams toward the borders.
19. Measure, cut, and sew the Fabric #4 outer border strips in the same fashion.
20. Quilt and bind as desired.

Autumn Leaves

9⅝" x 11⅝"

This pattern gives you a chance to use some of those lovely autumn scraps you may have on hand. One 6" scrap will provide the pieces for two leaf blocks. There are eighteen blocks in this quilt so using nine assorted prints works well. Add some muslin and a touch of embroidery, and the blocks are complete. This pattern is one of the few that incorporates the seam-and-cut method into the instructions. Since the sashings are only ⅛" wide when finished, small variations in the width will be noticeable. By cutting the sashings wider than needed, they can be cut to size after the first seam is sewn. Be sure to trim the sashing back after it has been sewn and checked, or it will be oversized when sewn to the next section.

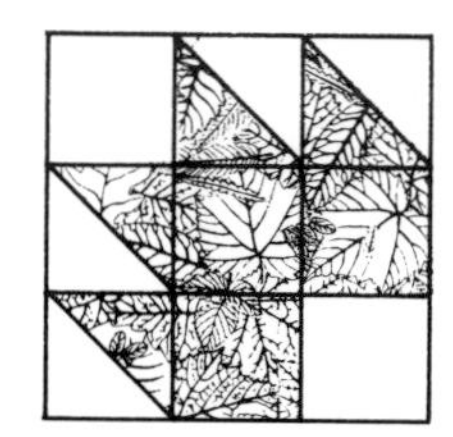

Autumn Leaf block
Finished size: 1⅛"

Cutting Requirements

Fabric #1: 9 assorted prints, each 6" square
Cut from each 6" square:
1 square, 3½" x 3½" (bias squares)
6 squares, ⅞" x ⅞" (leaf-block squares)

Fabric #2: Muslin, 15" x 18" piece
Cut: 9 squares, 3½" x 3½" (bias squares)
36 squares, ⅞" x ⅞" (leaf-block squares)
3 squares, 3¼" x 3¼" (oversized side triangles)
2 squares, 2¼" x 2¼" (oversized corner triangles)

Fabric #3: Dark green, 14" square
Cut: 2 strips, 1⅝" x 12" (short sashes)
4 strips, 1" x 12" (long sashes)
4 strips, 1" x 12" (inner border)
4 squares, 1" x 1" (corner squares for inner border)

Fabric #4: Dark brick print, 9" x 15" piece
Cut: 4 strips, 1½" x 12" (outer border)
4 squares, 1½" x 1½" (corner squares for outer border)

Backing and Binding: 12" x 14" piece, your fabric choice. To mimic model, use Fabric #4 and a rolled binding.

Assembly Instructions

1. Steam one of the 3½" print squares right sides together with one of the 3½" muslin squares. Cut 1⅛" bias strips from them and seam the strips into pairs. Seam the pairs to form multiple bias strata. Press the seams toward the print strips. Cut eight ⅞" bias squares from the strata. Do the same for each of the remaining 3½" print and muslin squares.
2. Lay the muslin squares, plain print squares, and bias squares on the work table and assemble each of the 18 blocks according to the diagram. Press seams in Rows 1 and 3 to the left. Press seams in Row 2 to the right. Blocks should measure 1⅝" square.

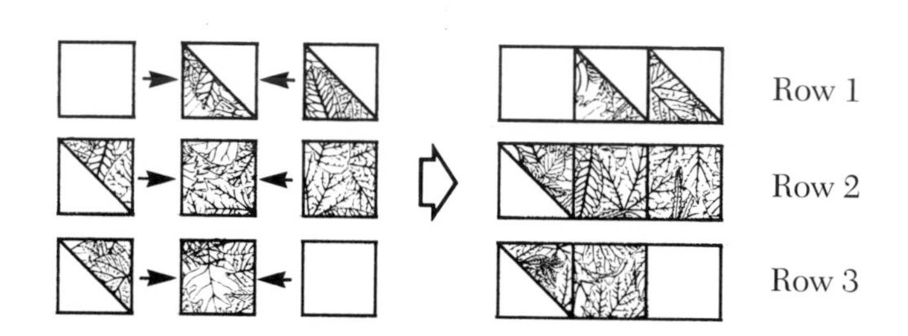

3. Arrange the pieced blocks on the table on point as they will be in the quilt. Play with the arrangement of the prints until they are in an order that pleases you. Try to evenly disperse the different color families. Once satisfied, pin your blocks in order to a piece of muslin to preserve the arrangement. It is important to keep your blocks in order on the table, so don't do any chain sewing right now. As you complete each step, pin the complete block back in place on the muslin.
4. Remove one block from the muslin. Lay the short end of a Fabric #3 sashing strip, 1⅝" x 12", on the upper right edge of the block as in the diagram. Sew the strip on. There will be a long length of strip extending to the left of the seam.

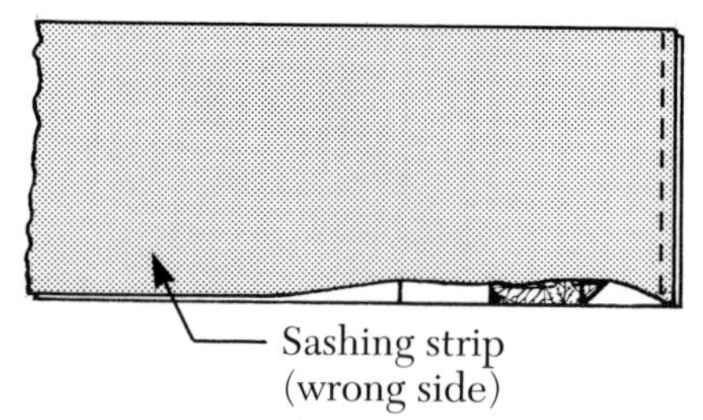

Sew short end of sashing strip to upper right edge of block. The sashing strip length will extend to the left.

5. Check the seam to make sure you sewed the strip onto the correct side. (It's surprisingly easy to get the block turned around.) Trim the seam allowance to ⅛" and press the seam toward the sashing strip.

6. On the right side, align your ruler with the block and cut sashing to 3/8" from block and sashing seam.

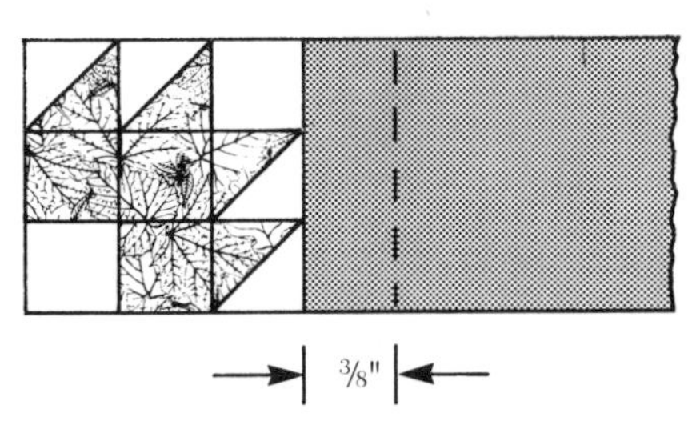

7. Pin the block back in its place on the muslin.
8. Follow Steps 4–7 for each leaf block, reusing the leftover sashing strip each time. When the strip is used up, use the second Fabric #3, 1 5/8" x 12" strip.
9. Once all the blocks have their right-hand short sashes sewn on, join them into rows as shown in the diagram. Sew each row one at a time and pin it back in place on the muslin before continuing.

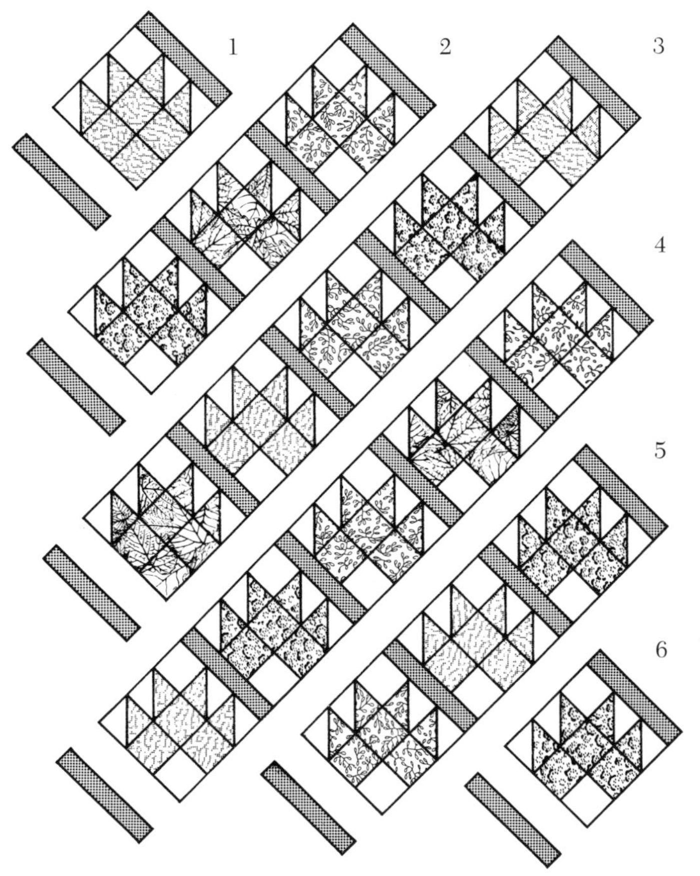

Piecing Diagram I

10. Using the leftover sashing strip from Step 8, add short sashes to the left side of the blocks on the ends of the rows as you did to the right side.
11. Each row in the diagram has been given a number. Please follow the rest of the instructions carefully so that you do not make the same mistakes I made the first time I assembled this quilt. Reserve one of the Fabric #3 strips, 1" x 12", for use later.
12. Lay the top edge of Row 3 on the long edge of one of the Fabric #3 sashing strips, 1" x 12". Sew the row to the strip as in the diagram. Check for accuracy before continuing.

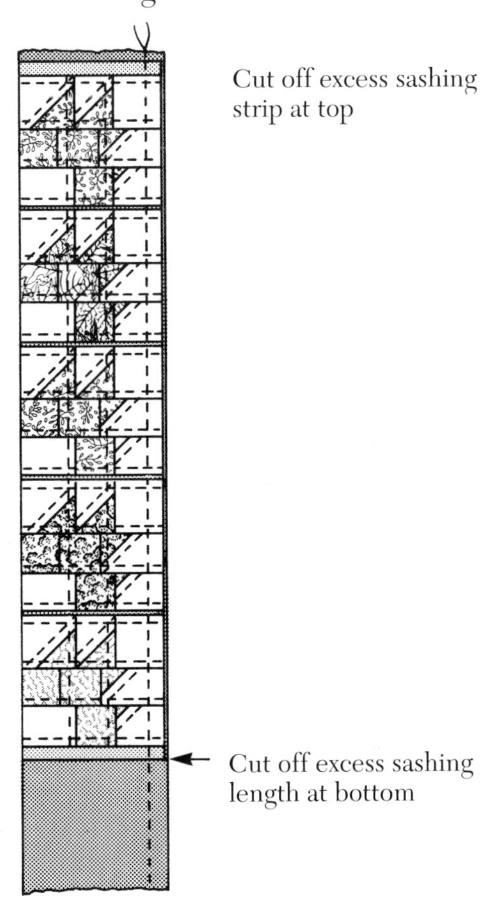

13. Remove the excess sashing length and trim the seam allowance to 1/8". Press the seam allowance toward the sashing and then cut the sashing width to 3/8" from the row/sashing seam.

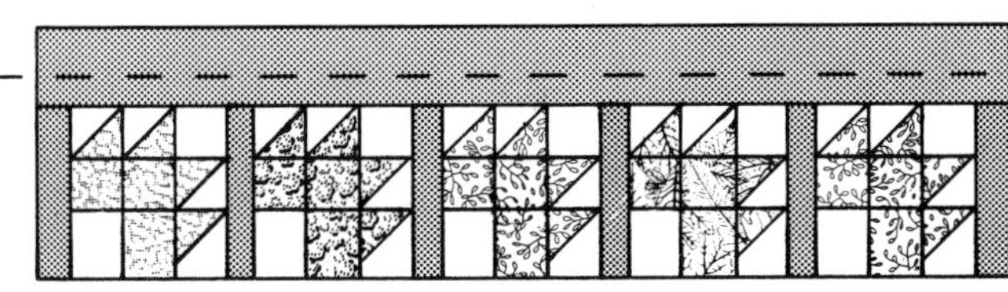
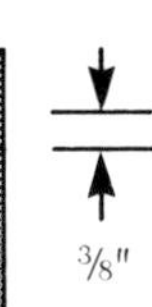

Trim sashing to 3/8" wide

14. Reusing the leftover sashing strip before starting on a fresh strip, continue adding long sashes to the rows in the following order to maximize strip usage:
    Row 4: Add sashing to the bottom edge
    Row 5: Add sashing to the bottom edge
    Row 2: Add sashing to the top edge
    Row 1: Add sashing to the top edge
    Row 6: Add sashing to the bottom edge
15. Cut the 3¼" muslin squares in half on both diagonals to create 10 quarter-square triangles for the sides. Lay these in place next to the rows as in the diagram.

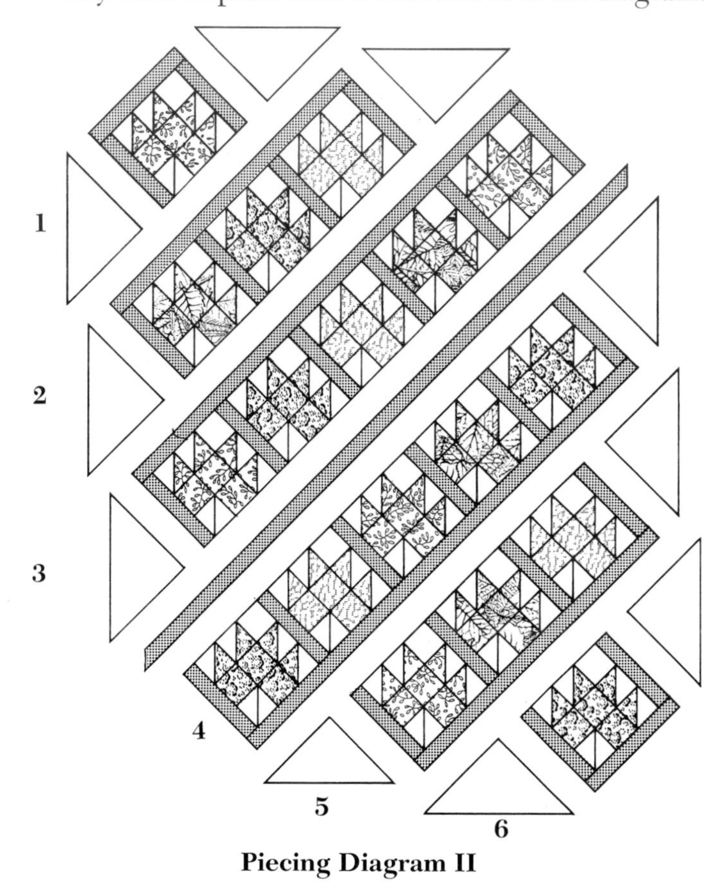

Piecing Diagram II

16. Sew the oversized side triangles in place, always beginning each seam at the right-angle corner of the triangle. This means that sometimes the sashing side will be face up when you sew and sometimes the triangle will be up. Please note that every row does not have a triangle on both ends. Press the seams toward the triangles.
17. On the wrong side of each long sashing, make sashing extension marks indicating where the short sashing seams lie.
18. Join Row 1 to Row 2, aligning the short sashing seams to the marks on the long sashing. Be careful not to stretch the bias edges of the triangles (the short sides). Remember, these triangles are still oversized at this point and will extend past the sashing length. Use pins to hold the sashing marks and triangle ends in place. Press the seams toward the sashings.
19. Join Row 3 and Row 2 in the same fashion.
20. Now, sew the reserved 1" x 12" sashing to the bottom of Row 3. Remove the excess length and trim it to ⅜" as with the other sashings. On the wrong side, make sashing extension marks to indicate where the short sashing seams lie.
21. Join Row 4 to Row 3 as you did the others. Then, join Rows 5 and 6 to the quilt. Press the seams toward the sashings.
22. Cut the 2¼" Fabric #2 squares in half on the diagonal to form 4 half-square triangles for the corner triangles. When sewing them to the quilt, be sure to center the point of the corner triangle with the center of the leaf blocks. Press the seams toward the corner triangles.
23. Trim the outer edges of the quilt to ¼" from the sashing corner points on all four sides. Using the ruler for accuracy, be sure to cut the corners square.
24. Cut two of the Fabric #3 inner border strips to fit the center length of the quilt. Cut the other two inner border strips to fit the center width. Seam the two long strips to the sides of the quilt. Press the seams toward the borders. Sew a border corner square to each end of the short strips and press the seams toward the strips. Sew these strips to the top and bottom of the quilt. Press the seams toward the border.
25. Attach the Fabric #4 outer border strips and corner squares in the same fashion.
26. Using one strand of brown floss, embroider a stem with the backstitch at the base of each leaf.

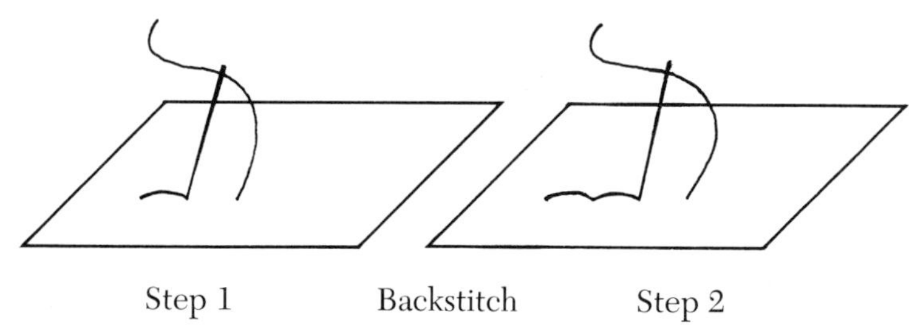

27. Quilt and bind as desired.

Autumn Leaves *by Donna Lynn Thomas, 1989, Frankfurt, West Germany, 9⅝" x 11⅝". This quilt brings to mind the crisp, breezy days of a fiery autumn.*

Moonlight Regatta

$9\frac{5}{8}$" x $8\frac{3}{8}$"

Every summer as a child, I used to spend many hours sitting at the Music Pier in Ocean City, N. J., with my grandfather. He would read his paper or, more often, listen to me chatter while we watched all the boats. At night, after walking the boards and visiting the amusements, I'd gaze toward the dark, moonlit ocean and wonder if all the boats I'd seen that day were still there. Moonlight Regatta was born from those memories. A simple, pieced sailboat pattern and a touch of appliqué create this tranquil seascape.

Traditional hand-basted appliqué as seen in the photo can be substituted with fusible webbings, freezer-paper appliqué, needle-turn, or whatever you prefer. Remember to mark your appliqué pieces on the right side of your fabric with a washable pencil and be sure to add a $\frac{3}{16}$" seam allowance around the markings when cutting out the appliqué pieces. Instructions are also included in this pattern for the seam-and-cut method. I hope you enjoy making this simple quilt—it's one of my favorites.

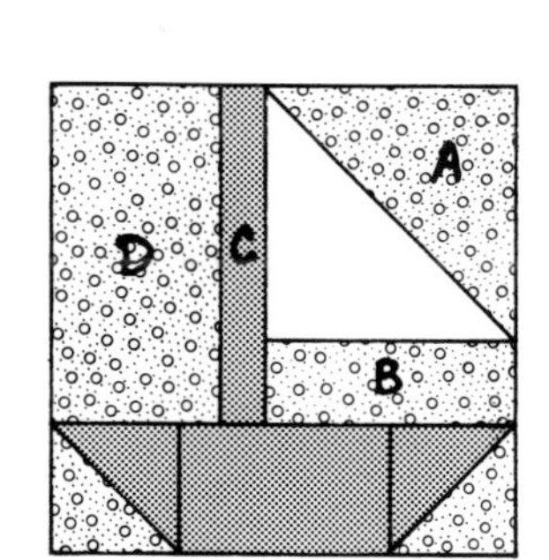

Sailboat block
Finished size: $1\frac{3}{8}$"
Units A, B, C, and D indicated

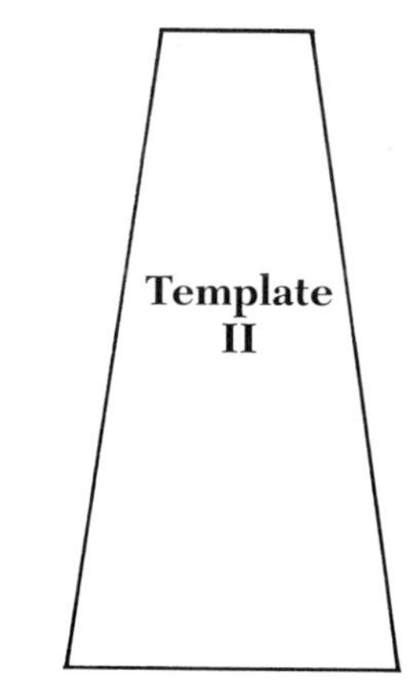

Fabric #5
Cut 1

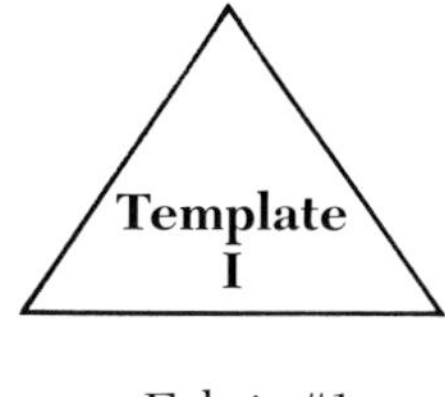

Fabric #1
Cut 1

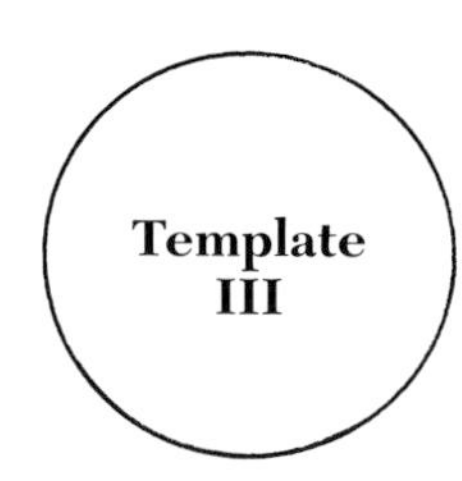

Fabric #6
Cut 1

Cutting Requirements

Fabric #1: Deep red, 12" square
Cut: 1 square, 5" x 5" (bias squares)
4 rectangles, $\frac{7}{8}$" x $1\frac{1}{8}$" (boat bottoms)
1 rectangle, $1\frac{1}{2}$" x 3" (Unit C)
4 strips, $1\frac{1}{4}$" x $11\frac{1}{2}$" (outer border)
1 Template I (lighthouse roof)

Fabric #2: Navy swirl, 9" x 14" piece
Cut: 1 square, $3\frac{1}{4}$" x $3\frac{1}{4}$" (sky)
2 squares, $1\frac{7}{8}$" x $1\frac{7}{8}$" (sky)
1 rectangle, $2\frac{1}{2}$" x $4\frac{5}{8}$" (sky)
1 square, 5" x 5" (bias squares)
1 square, $1\frac{1}{2}$" x $1\frac{1}{2}$" (Unit D)
1 rectangle, $1\frac{1}{4}$" x 1" (Unit B)

Fabric #3: Sea green print, 11" square
Cut: 1 square, $1\frac{7}{8}$" x $1\frac{7}{8}$" (sea)
3 rectangles, $1\frac{7}{8}$" x $3\frac{1}{4}$" (sea)
1 square, 5" x 5" (bias square)
1 strip, $1\frac{1}{2}$" x 5" (Unit D)
1 strip, $1\frac{1}{4}$" x 4" (Unit B)

Fabric #4: Brown print, 4" square
Cut: 1 square, 2" x 2" (bias square)
1 rectangle, $1\frac{1}{8}$" x $2\frac{5}{8}$" (shoreline)

Fabric #5: Gray/Mauve print, 2" x 3" scrap
Cut: 1 Template II (lighthouse)

Fabric #6: Pale gold, 2" square
Cut: 1 Template III (moon)

Fabric #7: Tan print, 5" square
Cut: 1 square, 5" x 5" (bias square)

Fabric #8: Tea-dyed star print, 9" x 12" piece
Cut: 4 strips, $1\frac{1}{2}$" x 11" (inner border)

Note: Fabrics #7 and #8 may be combined and cut from one print.

Backing and Binding: 12" x 13" piece, your fabric choice. To mimic model, use Fabric #1 and a rolled binding.

Assembly Instructions

1. Each of the pieces you have cut for bias squares will be cut first into strips of various sizes and then paired with other strips later, since very few bias squares are needed in any particular combination. Following are instructions on how many strips of what size are to be cut from each square indicated.

Begin by cutting the square in half on the diagonal and then cut the strips as you would normally. Cut the widest strips first and follow the order listed. Remember, this time the squares will not be paired with another fabric before cutting.

a. Fabric #7 (5" square): Cut 2 strips 1¼" wide.
b. Fabric #3 (5" square): Cut 1 strip 1¼" wide.
   Cut 2 strips 1" wide.
c. Fabric #2 (5" square): Cut 1 strip 1¼" wide.
   Cut 1 strip 1" wide.
   Reserve one waste corner.
d. Fabric #1 (5" square): Cut 3 strips 1" wide.
e. Fabric #4 (2" square): Cut in half on diagonal.

2. Combine the strips in the following manner and cut the indicated number and sizes of bias squares from the combinations. It is not necessary for the strips to be the same length.
   a. 1¼" strips: Fabric #7 + Fabric #3
      Press seams to Fabric #3.
      Cut: 3 bias squares, 1¼" x 1¼" (Unit A—sails)
   b. 1¼" strips: Fabric #7 + Fabric #2
      Press seams to Fabric #2.
      Cut: 1 bias square, 1¼" x 1¼" (Unit A—sail)
   c. 1" strips: Fabric #3 + Fabric #1—2 sets
      Press seams to Fabric #1.
      Cut: 6 bias squares, ⅞" x ⅞" (boats)
   d. 1" strips: Fabric #2 + Fabric #1
      Press seams to Fabric #1.
      Cut: 2 bias squares, ⅞" x ⅞" (boats)
   e. Fabric #2 (waste corner) + Fabric #4 (2" triangle)
      Press seams to Fabric #4.
      Cut: 1 bias square, 1⅛" x 1⅛" (shoreline)

   Note: There are two sailboat block colorations—one fabric for the three sailboats in the sea and another fabric for the sailboat on the blue horizon. Be sure to use the right color fabrics for each sailboat and guard against mixing them up.

3. Align the 1¼" width of the Fabric #3 Unit B piece with the bottom of a sea sail. Seam it to the sail and press the seam toward Unit B. Trim Unit B to ½" from the seam. Do the same with the other sails in the sea.

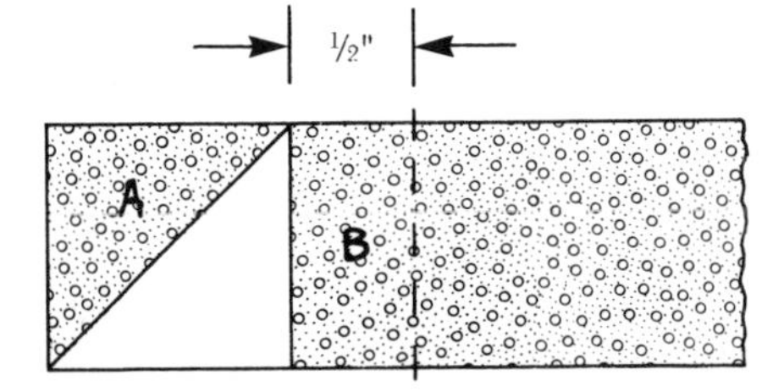

Cut Unit B to ½" from seam

4. Add the Fabric #2 Unit B rectangle to the bottom of the sky sail. Align the 1¼" width with the bottom of the sail and press and trim in the same fashion as for the sea sails.

5. Align the 1½" width of the Fabric #1 Unit C rectangle with the left side of any sail. Seam it to the sail. Press the seams toward Unit C. Cut Unit C to ⅜" from the seam.

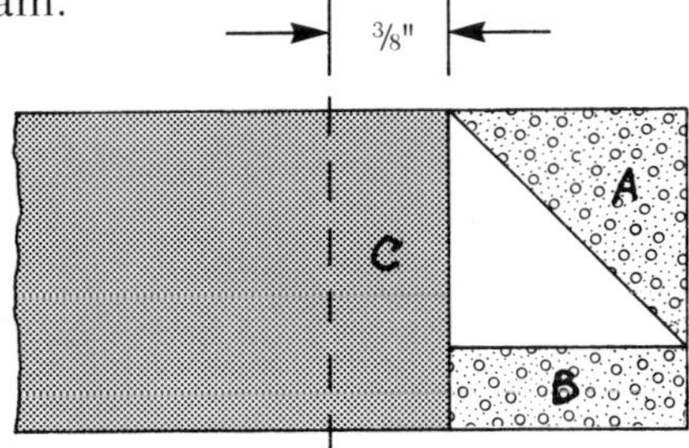

Cut Unit C to ⅜" from seam

6. Add Unit C to the rest of the sails in the same fashion.

7. Lay the 1½" width of the Fabric #3 Unit D strip to the left of one of the sailboats in the sea. Seam and press the seam toward Unit D. Trim Unit D to ¾" from the seam.

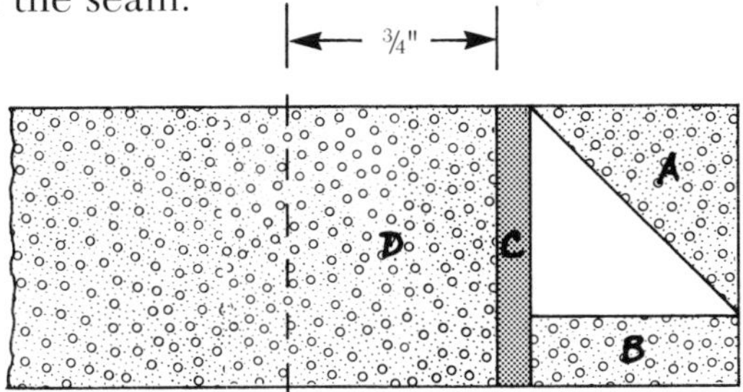

Cut Unit D to ¾" from seam

8. Do the same for the remaining sailboats in the sea.

9. Using the 1½" Fabric #2 square, attach Unit D to the sailboat in the sky. Sew, press, and trim in the same way as you did for the sailboats in the sea.

10. Attach the appropriate bias squares to each of the 4 Fabric #1 boat bottoms to make 3 boats in the sea and 1 boat on the horizon.

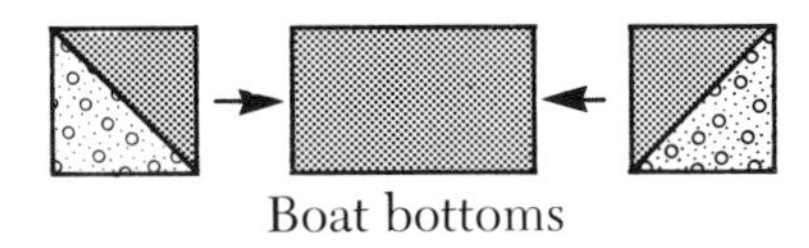
Boat bottoms

11. Seam tops of the sailboat blocks to their corresponding bottoms. Press the seams in either direction.

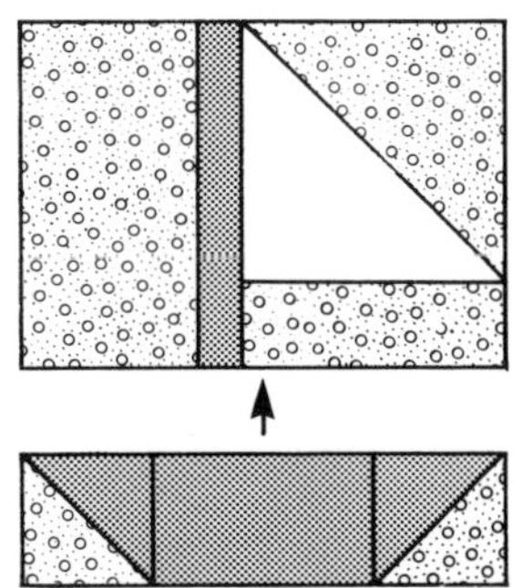

12. Prepare the lighthouse base by turning under the sides and hand basting on the chalk lines. The ends may be left unturned.

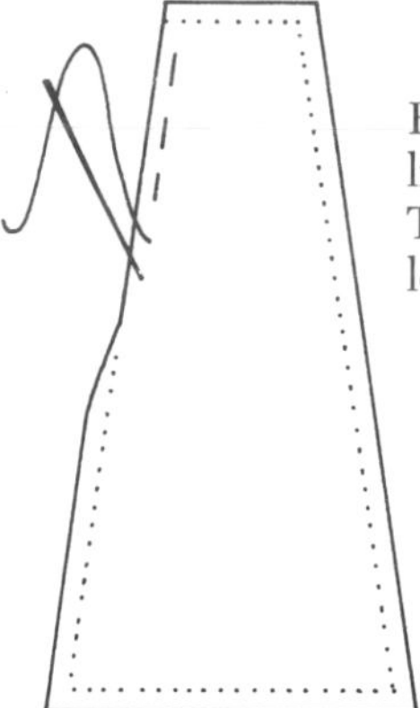

Roll edge under on chalk line and baste in place. The short ends can be left unbasted.

13. Trim the bottom edge of the lighthouse to an even 3/16" from the pencil line and align it with the bottom of the right side of the 3¼" Fabric #2 square. Shift it so that it is ¾" in from the left-hand raw edge of the square.
14. Using a matching thread, blind hemstitch it in place, making sure that it is upright and not leaning.

Blind hemstitch

Moonlight Regatta *by Donna Lynn Thomas, 1989, Frankfurt, West Germany, 9⅝" x 8⅜". Textured fabrics are the perfect accents for this quilt, which is reminiscent of warm, summer evenings by the ocean.*

15. Seam the shoreline bias square to the right side of the shoreline rectangle. Press the seam toward the rectangle. Seam this unit to the bottom of the lighthouse square.
16. Seam a 1⅞" sky square to either side of the sailboat on the horizon. Press the seams toward the plain squares. Seam the Fabric #2 rectangle, 2½" x 4⅝", to the top of the sailboat and sky unit. Press seam up.
17. Seam the sailboat and sky unit to the lighthouse unit and press the seam toward the lighthouse unit.
18. Form two sea rows using the remaining large sea rectangles, sailboats, and square. Join them to form the lower half of the quilt. Press the seams toward the plain pieces.
19. Join the two halves together. Press the seam up.
20. Following the directions for straight-set borders on page 23, attach the Fabric #8 inner border strips.
21. Attach the Fabric #1 outer border strips in the same fashion.
22. Baste under the edges of the moon and lighthouse roof. Position them where you want them and blind hemstitch them in place with matching threads.
23. Quilt and bind as desired.

Note: I used a fish quilting design in the sea area and quilted random cloudlike formations in the sky. The rest of the center of the quilt was quilted in the ditch. The star design was quilted in the inner border to repeat the nighttime theme. These designs and others may be found on pages 86–87.

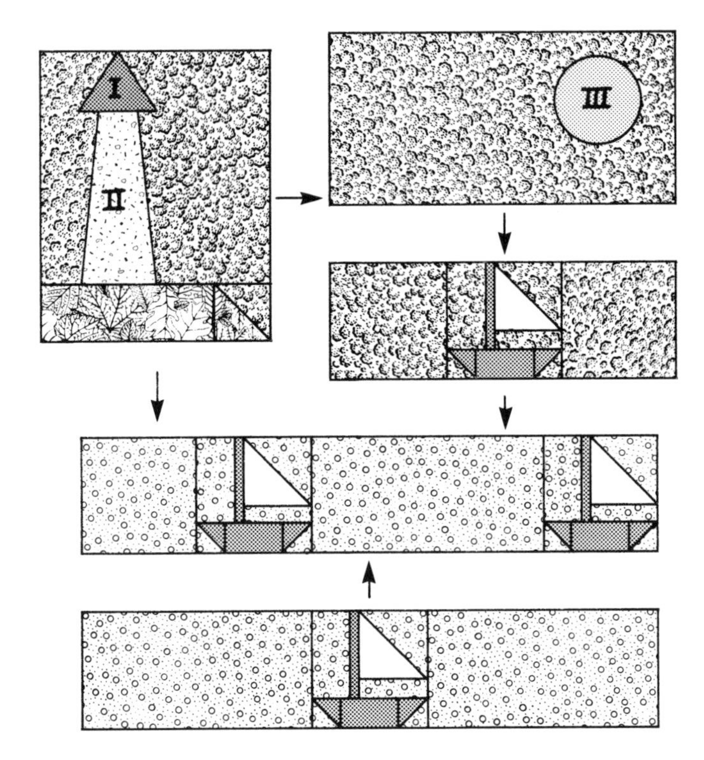

Tea Rose

11¾" x 11¾"

Tea Rose is an old-fashioned, pieced floral pattern. It's simple to construct but please be careful of the bias edges. Done in miniature with delicate pastels and lots of quilting, this pattern is a delight to the eye. You can almost feel warm summer breezes and the perfume of a rose garden in the air!

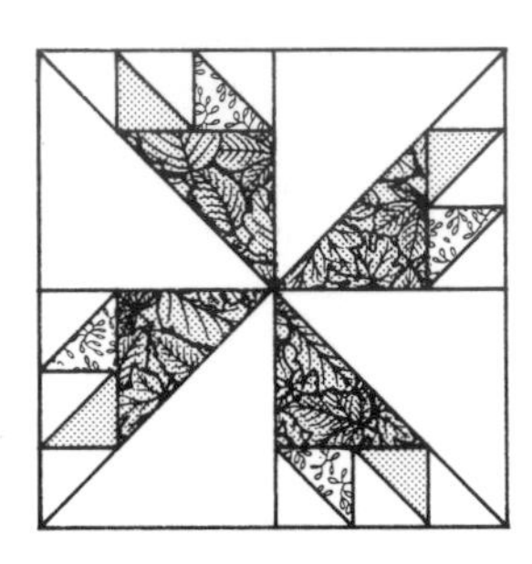

Tea Rose block
Finished size: 2¼"

Cutting Requirements

Fabric #1: Pink solid, 12" square
Cut: 1 square, 6" x 6" (bias squares)
4 strips, ¾" x 8" (inner border)

Fabric #2: Medium rose print, 8" square
Cut: 1 square, 6" x 6" (bias squares)
4 squares, ¾" x ¾" (inner border corner squares)

Fabric #3: Green print, 9" square
Cut: 10 squares, 1⅝" x 1⅝" (flower bases)

Fabric #4: Muslin, 18" x 22" piece (fat-quarter)
Cut: 8 squares, 2¾" x 2¾" (plain blocks, corner squares)
10 squares, 2" x 2" (large Tea Rose triangles)
4 strips, 2¾" x 7¾" (outer border)
2 squares, 6" x 6" (bias squares)
10 squares, 1¼" x 1¼" (small Tea Rose triangles)

Backing and binding: 14" square, your fabric choice. To mimic model, use Fabric #4 and a rolled binding.

Assembly Instructions

1. Steam a 6" Fabric #4 square right sides together with each of the pink 6" squares (Fabrics #1 and #2). Cut each pair into 1⅛" bias strips, seam into multiple bias strata, and press seams toward the prints. Cut ⅞" bias squares from each combination; you will need 20 of each.
2. Cut the 2" Fabric #4 squares in half on the diagonal to form 20 large half-square triangles.
3. Cut the 1¼" Fabric #4 squares in half on the diagonal to form 20 small half-square triangles.
4. Cut the 1⅝" Fabric #3 squares in half on the diagonal to form 20 half-square triangles for the flower bases.
5. Using the ⅞" bias squares and the half-square triangles from Step 3, assemble 20 bias-square rows as in the diagram. Press seams toward the half-square triangles.

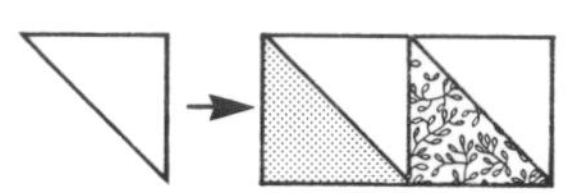

6. Seam the flower bases to the bottom of the bias-square rows as in the diagram. Press the seams toward the bases.

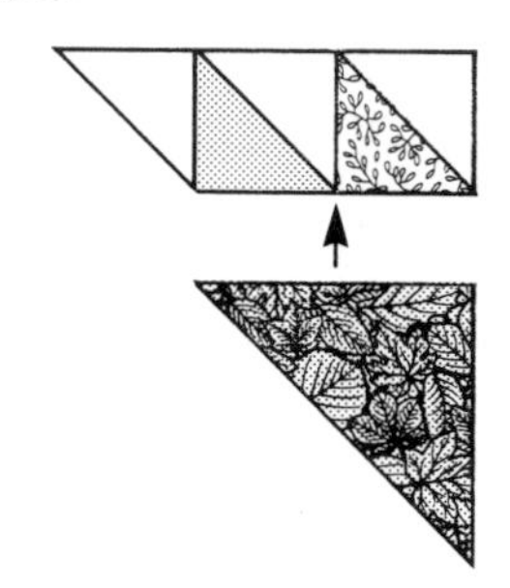

7. Trim the edges to ¼" from the points, if necessary, and seam the large Fabric #4 triangles from step 2 to the long edge of the rose unit to form 20 squares. Press seams toward the large triangles.

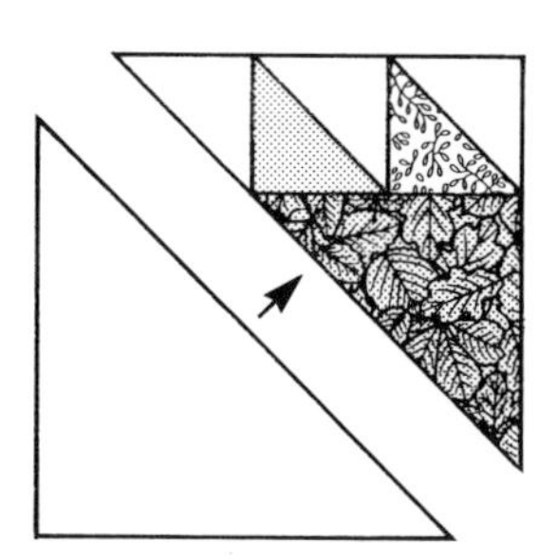

8. Join four rose squares together pinwheel fashion to complete 5 blocks. Press seams in the rows toward the large triangle and press the center block seam in any direction.
9. Seam the rose blocks together alternately with the 2¾" plain blocks to form 3 rows as in the photo. Press the seams toward the plain blocks.
10. Join the rows together to form the quilt body. Press the seams in either direction.
11. Measure and cut the Fabric #1 inner border strips to fit the center width of the quilt. Attach the side

borders. Press the seams toward the border strips.

12. Add the Fabric #2 corner squares to either end of the two remaining strips. Seam them to the top and bottom of the quilt. Press the seams toward the border strips.
13. Attach the large Fabric #4 outer borders in the same fashion.
14. Quilt and bind as desired.

***Tea Rose** by Donna Lynn Thomas, 1988, Frankfurt, West Germany, 11¾" x 11¾". Delicate pastels and lots of quilting in the plain blocks provide a visual feast in this miniature. You can almost smell the roses!*

Little St. Nick

6⅞" x 9⅞"

The inspiration for this design came after many failed attempts at drawing a Santa for a Christmas decoration. One day, while I was frantically making another attempt, one of my sons asked for help assembling a little Lego™ Santa kit his grandmother had sent him. As we worked, it dawned on me that the building blocks would lend themselves well to quilt designs and, thus, with a few changes, Little St. Nick was born.

The fancy pieced border in the photo may be eliminated, if you desire. Without the border, only sixteen bias squares are needed, speeding the assembly time if you are working on this the night before Christmas! Single Santas with ribbon hangers make wonderful gifts, magnets, or gift tie-ons.

St. Nick block
Finished size: 1½" x 3"

Cutting Requirements

Fabric #1: Red print, 13" x 19" piece
Cut: 2 squares, 9" x 9" (bias squares)
1 strip, ¾" x 10" (Strata I)
1 strip, 1" x 6" (Strata II)
1 strip, ¾" x 6" (Strata II)
4 squares, ⅞" x ⅞" (border squares)

Fabric #2: Pink solid, 3" x 12" piece
Cut: 1 strip, ¾" x 10" (Strata I)
1 strip, 1" x 6" (Strata II)

Fabric #3: Muslin, 5" x 12" piece
Cut: 2 strips, ¾" x 6" (Strata II)
1 strip, ⅝" x 10" (Strata I)
1 strip, ⅞" x 6" (Strata II)

Fabric #4: Green print, 5" x 12" piece
Cut: 4 strips, ⅞" x 12" (sashings)

Fabric #5: Black solid, 9" square
Cut: 1 strip, ⅞" x 6" (Strata II)
1 strip, ⅝" x 6" (Strata II)
4 strips, 1½" x 9" (outer border)

Fabric #6: Tan solid, 13" x 18" piece
Cut: 2 squares, 9" x 9" (bias squares)
1 strip, 1⅜" x 10" (Strata I)
8 rectangles, ⅞" x 1⅝" (arm units)

Backing and Binding: 9" x 12" piece, your fabric choice. To mimic model, use Fabric #5 and a rolled binding.

Assembly Instructions

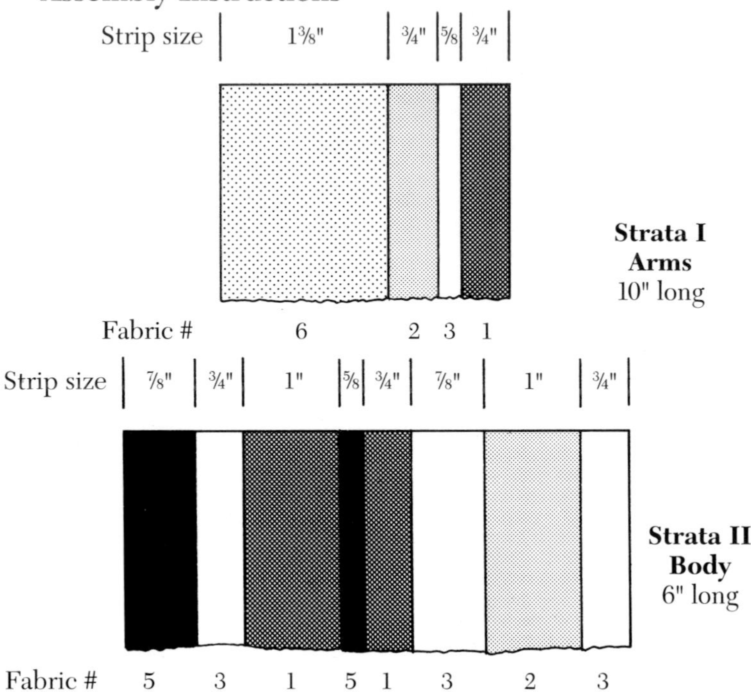

1. Assemble Strata I and Strata II according to the diagrams. Be careful not to mix up the strips since they are similar in size. Also, remember to trim and press the seams as you go to reduce the bulk under the presser foot. Press the seams in Strata I toward the Fabric #1 end. Press the seams in Strata II toward the Fabric #3 end except for the center muslin strip, which should have both seams pressed toward it.
2. Cut eight ⅞" segments from Strata I and four 1¼" segments from Strata II.
3. Steam the 9" Fabric #1 and Fabric #6 squares right sides together. Cut 1⅛" bias strips from them and seam them into pairs. Press the seams toward the

dark fabric except for the two smallest bias strata, which should be pressed toward the light fabric. Seam the pairs into multiple bias strata.

4. Cut 7/8" bias squares from the bias strips; you will need 76. Sixty bias squares will be used for the sawtooth border and the rest for the St. Nick blocks. Set aside 4 bias squares that have their seams pressed toward the light fabric.
5. Sew each of the 4 reserved bias squares to 1 of the other bias squares to form St. Nick's hats. If you use bias squares with opposing seam allowances, the diagonal seams are more likely to form an exact point where they meet. Press the center seam toward the bias square that has its seam pressed toward the light fabric.

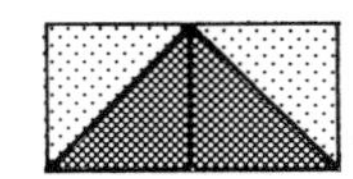

6. Sew a hat to the muslin end of each Strata II segment. Press the seam toward the strata.
7. Sew a bias square to the end of each Fabric #6 rectangle, 7/8" x 1⅝". Note that 4 arm units require the bias-square shoulders to face in one direction while the other 4 face the other way. Press the seams toward the rectangles.

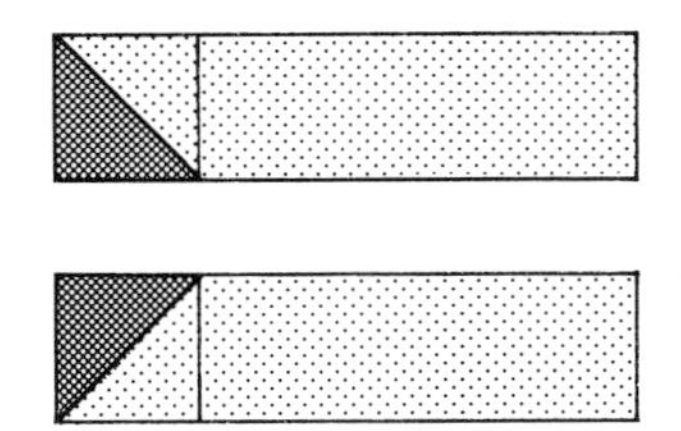

8. Sew the Fabric #1 end of a Strata I segment to the other side of the bias square. Press the seam toward the strata.

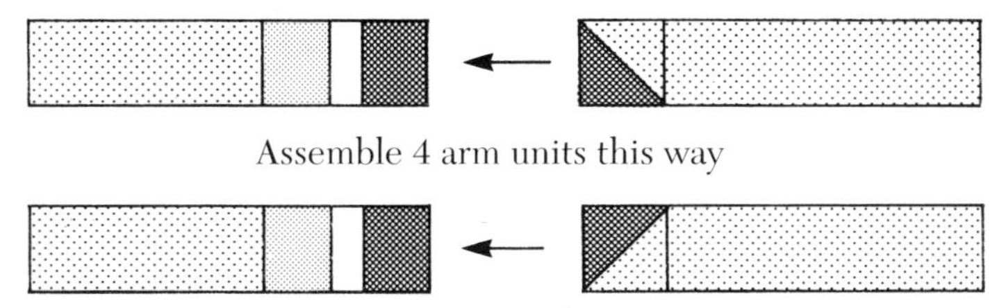

9. Sew an arm unit to either side of each body segment. Be sure to sew the correct arm to the correct side of the body so that St. Nick's shoulders slope away from his body. Press the seams toward the center.
10. From the Fabric #4 strips, cut 2 sashing strips to fit the center length of the blocks. Join the blocks into pairs with the sashing strips between them. Press the seams toward the sashing.

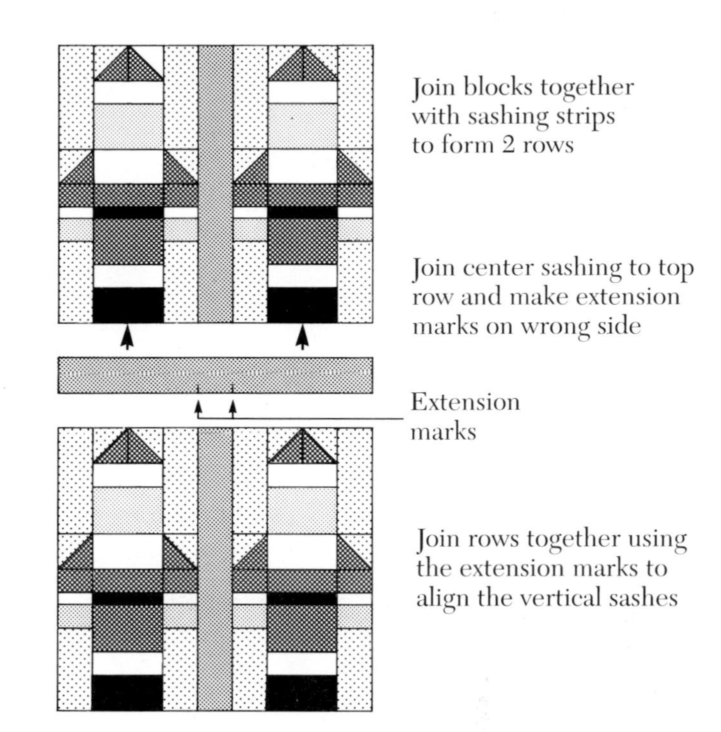

11. Cut another sashing strip to fit the center width of the two rows. Sew it to the bottom of the top row. Press the seam toward the sashing. On the wrong side, make extension marks to indicate where the interior sashing seams lie.
12. Aligning the pencil marks with the short sashing seams of the row, join the bottom row to the center sashing. Press the seam toward the sashing.
13. Cut 2 sashing strips to fit the center length of the quilt. Sew them to the sides of the quilt. Press the seams toward the sashings.
14. Cut 2 sashings to fit the center width of the quilt. Sew them to the top and bottom and press seams toward the sashing.
15. Sew bias squares together to form strips as in the diagram. Press seams toward the center plain square.

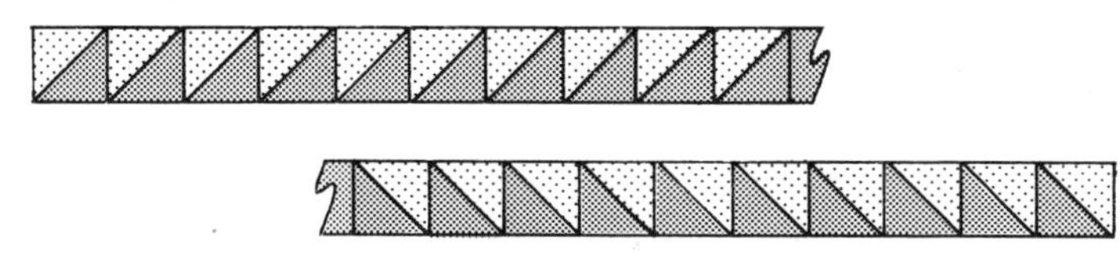

Side Borders
Assemble 2. Press seams toward center.

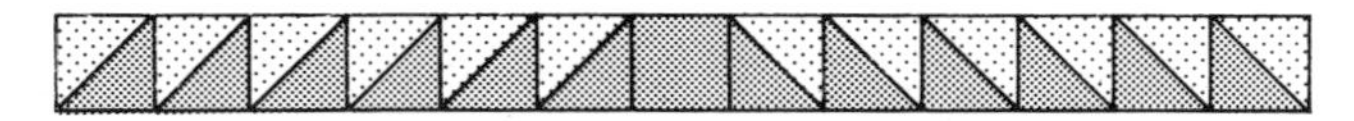

Top and Bottom Borders
Assemble 2. Press all seams toward the center except the 2 end bias squares.

16. Aligning the center border square with the center sashing strip, join the side strips to the sashing. Press the seams toward the sashing.

17. Aligning the center border square with the center sashing, join the top and bottom borders to the sashing. Use the opposing seams at the junction of the two borders to make a tight intersection. Press seams toward the sashing strips.
18. Following the directions for straight-set borders on page 23, attach the Fabric #5 outer border strips.
19. Add eyes and nose with permanent markers (test them first on scrap fabric) or embroider them with French knots. Use 2 strands of black floss for the eyes and 2 strands of red floss for the nose. To help with placement of the knots, make a plastic template the size of the face. Mark the eyes and nose on the template where you want them and punch holes through the marks with a 1/8" hole punch or hot awl. You now have a consistent guide for lightly marking St. Nick's face before you embroider or draw his eyes and nose.

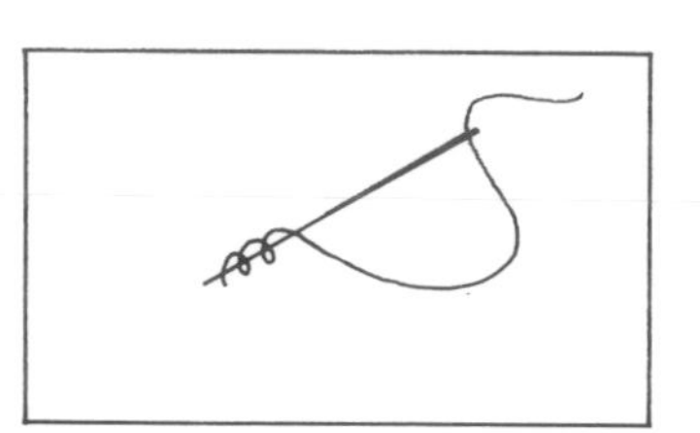

French Knot

Wrap the floss around the point of the needle

Pull the needle to the underside and secure it with a backstitch under the knot

20. Quilt and bind as desired.

Little St. Nick *by Donna Lynn Thomas, 1988, Frankfurt, West Germany, 6⅞" x 9⅞". A sawtooth border accents the little stylized Santas for a festive Christmas quilt.*

Freedom's Home

9¼" x 12¼"

House blocks are perennial favorites because they remind us of so many wonderful things. Living overseas for a few years is a terrific opportunity that my family and I would not want to miss. We enjoy all there is to see and do as well as the people we meet. Even so, there are times when we miss our home country. There is nothing like a far-off view to truly appreciate what we experience in the States as nowhere else in the world. This quilt means a lot to me right now, but I'm just as sure that someday I will have to make a quilt to quiet the sadness of leaving my European friends behind.

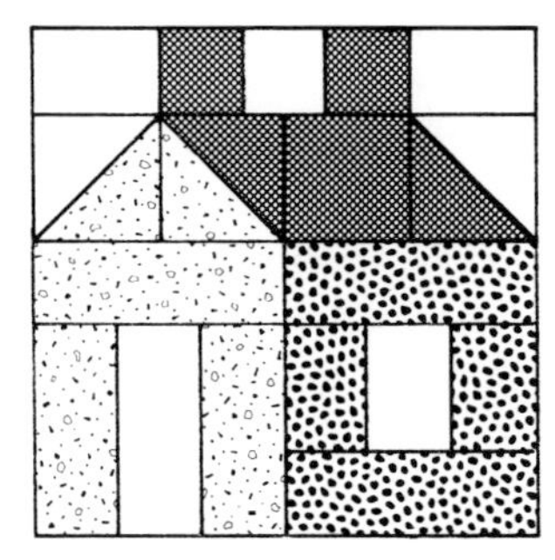

House block
Finished size: 1½"

Star (border)
Finished size: ¾"

Cutting Requirements

Fabric #1: Red print, 9" x 15" piece
Cut:
- 2 strips, ¾" x 8" (chimney—Strata I)
- 2 squares, 3½" x 3½" (roof bias squares)
- 1 strip, ⅞" x 9" (roof)
- 4 strips, ¾" x 14" (border stripes—Strata IV)

Fabric #2: Tea-dyed star print, 18" square
Cut:
- 2 strips, ⅞" x 8" (chimney—Strata I)
- 2 strips, ¾" x 8" (chimney—Strata I, window—Strata III)
- 2 squares, 3½" x 3½" (roof bias squares)
- 1 strip, ¾" x 11" (door—Strata II)
- 2 strips, ¾" x 14" (border stripes—Strata IV)
- 2 strips, ¾" x 9" (star squares)
- 1 square, 9" x 9" (star bias squares)
- 7 squares, 2" x 2" (alternate plain blocks)
- 4 squares, ⅞" x ⅞" (inner border corner squares)
- 2 strips, ⅞" x 9" (inner border)
- 2 strips, ⅞" x 6" (inner border)

Fabric #3: Medium blue print, 13" x 16" piece
Cut:
- 2 squares, 3½" x 3½" (roof bias squares)
- 2 strips, ¾" x 11" (door—Strata II)
- 1 strip, ¾" x 14" (door-top strip)
- 4 squares, 1½" (outer border corner squares)
- 2 strips, 1½" x 11" (outer borders)
- 2 strips, 1½" x 8" (outer borders)

Fabric #4: Dark blue print, 18" square
Cut:
- 1 square, 9" x 9" (star bias squares)
- 2 strips, ¾" x 14" (windows)
- 2 strips, ¾" x 8" (window—Strata III)
- 5 strips, ¾" x 14" (star squares)

Backing and Binding: 11" x 14" piece, your fabric choice. To mimic model, use Fabric #3 and a rolled binding.

Assembly Instructions

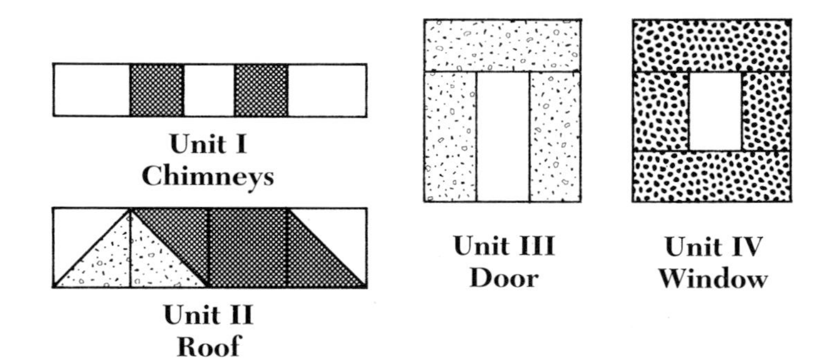

1. The House blocks are assembled in 4 separate units as illustrated in the diagram.
2. Begin by assembling Strata I as shown in the diagram. Press the seams away from the center strip toward the edge of the strata. Cut ¾" segments from the strata to form completed chimney units; you will need 8.

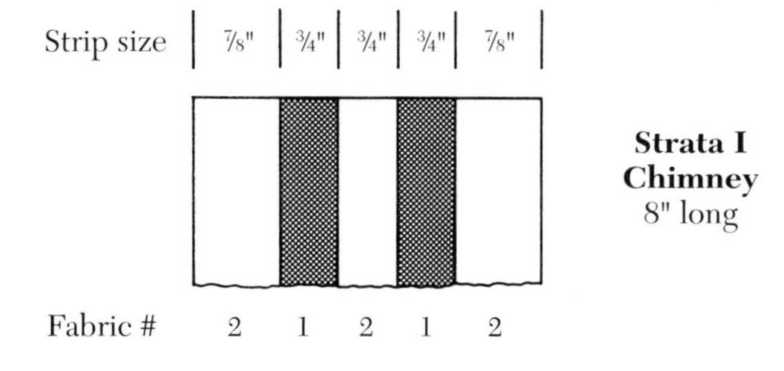

3. The roof unit is composed of a single square and 3 bias squares. Steam one 3½" Fabric #1 square right sides together with one 3½" Fabric #2 square. Cut 1⅛" bias strips and seam them into pairs. Join the like-size pairs into multiple bias strata. Press the

seams toward Fabric #1. Cut ⅞" bias squares from the bias strata; you will need 8.

4. Steam the other 3½" Fabric #1 square with one of the 3½" Fabric #3 squares. Assemble multiple bias strata as in step 3. Press seams toward Fabric #1. Cut ⅞" bias squares; you will need 8.
5. Steam the remaining 3½" Fabric #2 and #3 squares together. Assemble multiple bias strata as in step 3. Press seams toward Fabric #3. Cut ⅞" bias squares; you will need 8.
6. Cut the Fabric #1 strip, ⅞" x 9", into ⅞" squares; you will need 8. Lay the roof units out and sew them together as in the diagram. Press the seams toward the center plain square.

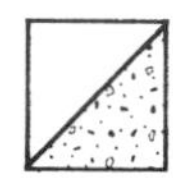 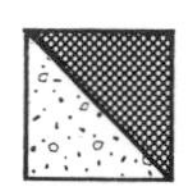  

7. Matching seams, join the roof and chimney units together.
8. Assemble Strata II as in the diagram. Press the seams toward the darker strips. Cut 1⅛" segments from the strata; you will need 8.

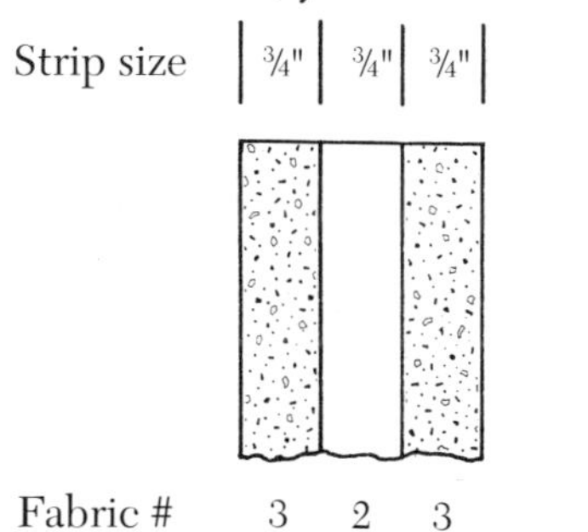

Strata II
Door
11" long

9. Chain sew the segments to the remaining ¾" x 14" Fabric #3 strip as in the diagram. Cut apart. Press the seams toward the strata. These are the doors.

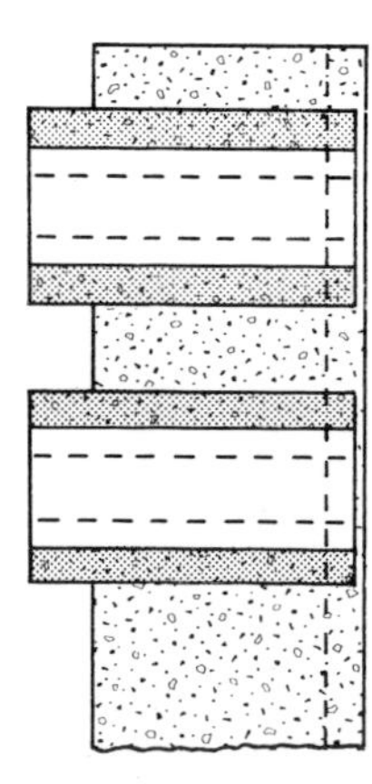

10. Assemble Strata III as in the diagram. Use the Fabric #2 and #4 strips, ¾" x 8". Press the seams toward Fabric #4. Cut ⅞" segments; you will need 8. Chain sew the segments to a Fabric #4 strip, ¾" x 14", as in step 9. Cut apart and press the seams toward the single strip.

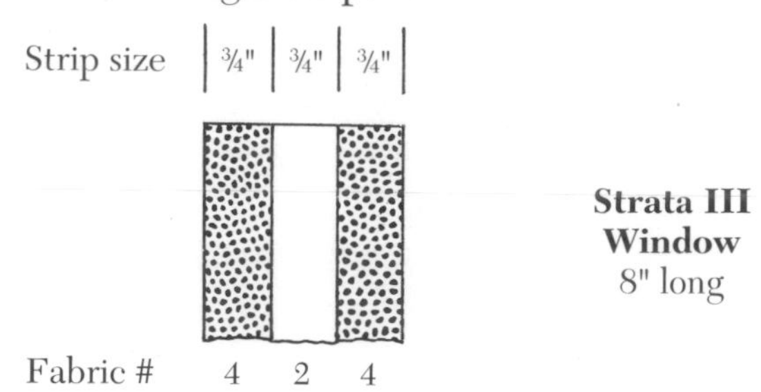

11. Chain sew the other end of the strata segments to the other Fabric #4 strip, ¾" x 14", in the same fashion. Cut apart and press the seam toward the strip. These are the window units.
12. Aligning the seams, sew the door and window units together. Press seams toward the door units.
13. Join the two halves of the house blocks together. Press the seams toward the lower half of the house.
14. Join the House blocks into rows alternately with the 2" Fabric #2 plain blocks as in the photo. Press seams toward the plain blocks. Join the rows to form the quilt center. Press rows in either direction.
15. Following the directions for straight-set borders on page 23, attach the Fabric #2 inner border strips and corner squares.
16. Assemble 2 sets of Strata IV as in the diagram. Press the seams toward the light fabric. Cut strata into 1¼" segments; you will need 20. These are the stripes in the stars-and-stripes border.

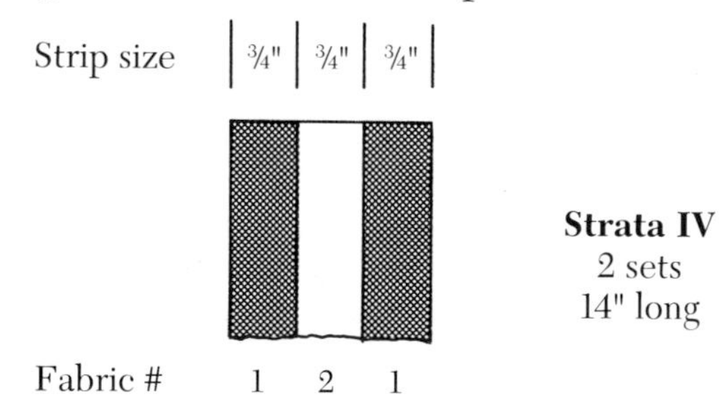

17. Steam the two 9" Fabric #2 and Fabric #4 squares right sides together into pairs. Cut 1" bias strips from them and seam them into multiple bias strata. Press the seams toward Fabric #4. Cut bias strata into ¾" bias squares; you will need 80.
18. Cut the 2 Fabric #2 strips, ¾" x 9", into ¾" squares; you will need 20. Cut the 5 Fabric #4 strips, ¾" x 14", into ¾" squares; you will need 80.
19. Lay the bias squares and plain squares on the table as in the diagram. Join the units to form rows. Press the seams toward the plain blocks. Join the rows to form 20 stars. Press the seams toward the center of the block.

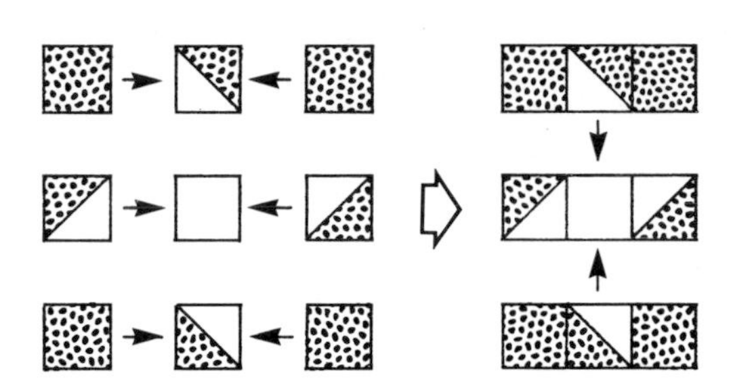

20. Join 5 star blocks alternately with 6 stripe blocks; make sure you have a stripe block on both ends. Assemble another strip in the same fashion. Press the seams toward the stripe blocks. Sew them to the sides of the quilt. Press the seams toward the center of the quilt.
21. Join 5 star blocks alternately with 4 stripe blocks; make sure you have a star block on both ends. Assemble another strip in the same fashion. Press the seams toward the stripe blocks. Sew the border strips to the top and bottom of the quilt. Press the seams toward the center of the quilt.
22. Following the directions for straight-set borders on page 23, attach the Fabric #3 outer border strips and corner squares.
23. Quilt and bind as desired.

Freedom's Home *by Donna Lynn Thomas, 1989, Frankfurt, West Germany, 9¼" x 12¼". Patriotic influences abound in this little house quilt with its stars-and-stripes border.*

Section III:

SIDE-BY-SIDE TRIANGLES

Side-by-side triangles are two quarter-square triangles that are joined to each other on one of their short legs rather than along the hypotenuse. An example of side-by-side triangles can be seen in the Ohio Star block.

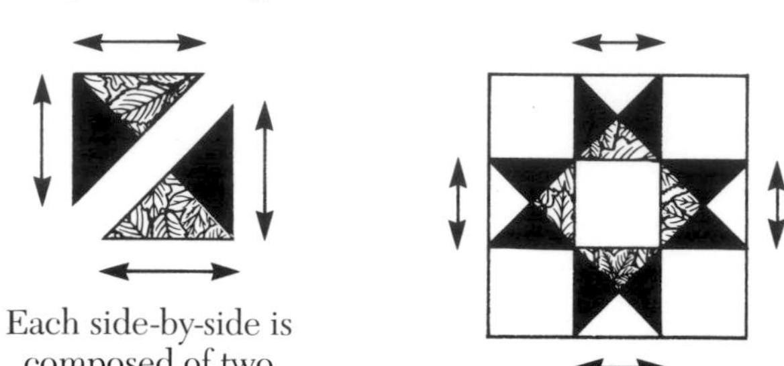

Each side-by-side is composed of two quarter-square triangles

Two side-by-sides joined together form a square

Note that in a block such as the Ohio Star, the long edges of the four triangles making up the square should be on the straight of grain as indicated by the arrows in the diagram.

This section will show you a quick method for making presewn side-by-side triangles. The technique is a variation on bias-square construction and, even though all the side-by-side patterns in *Small Talk* require the straight of grain to be on the long triangle edges, you will also learn how to adjust the method to produce units with the bias on the long edges.

Basic Concept

Bias squares are joined together along the hypotenuse of the triangles. Side-by-side triangles, however, are joined together on a short edge. If you cut a presewn bias square in half on the diagonal, you end up with two sets of side-by-side triangles. Each set is the mirror image of its mate.

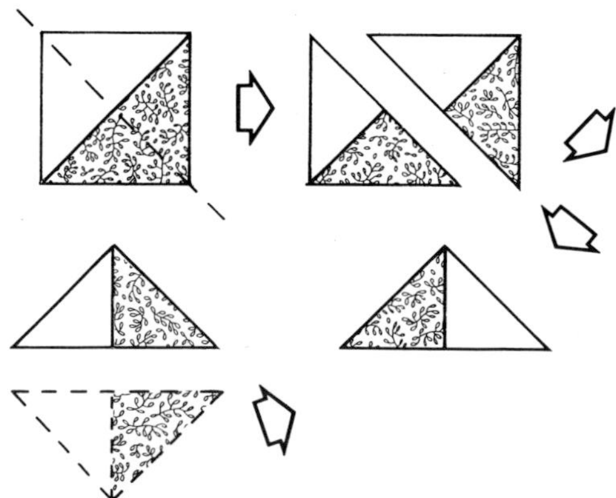

The one disadvantage to making side-by-side triangles in this manner is that both mirror-image versions are produced for each bias square. If the pattern you wish to make requires only one version, you will have an equal number of leftover opposite versions. You can use the leftovers to make a miniature scrap quilt or a Windmill quilt. What's nice about the Windmill block is that you can use either version to construct the block.

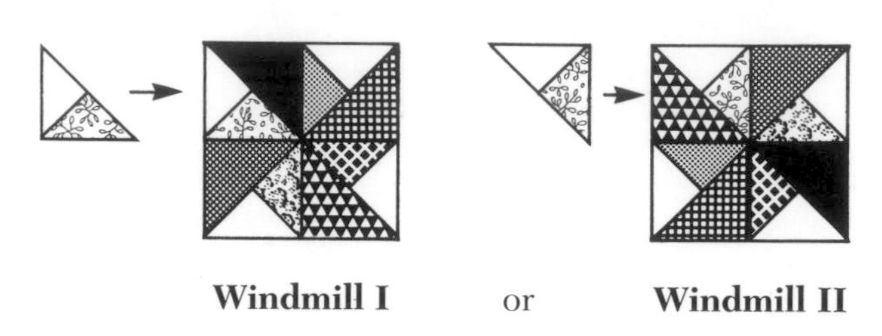

Windmill I or **Windmill II**

You may also want to make a mirror-image version of the original quilt and have two quilts for half the work.

Before you start cutting, you need to know:

1. The desired finished size of the side-by-side unit's long edge
2. The size of the bias square you will need to cut to yield the correct size of the side-by-side unit
3. The width of the bias strip you will need to cut to make the bias squares

Determining Side-by-Side Size

If you are drafting your own pattern, the finished size of the long edge can be determined by measuring. If you are making a pattern in this book, the directions will guide you. Other times, the size can be determined logically. If you are constructing a Windmill block, which is a traditional Four-Patch pattern, the finished size of the side-by-side long edge is going to be half the size of the finished block.

Determining the Size of the Bias Square

Think of the side-by-side units as half-square triangles that you will be cutting from a square. If you are making half-square triangles (see page 16), you may remember that the magic number to add to the finished size of the triangle is ⅞". The same number applies to cutting bias squares large enough to produce side-by-sides. Add ⅞" to the desired finished size of the side-by-side long edge and cut a bias square that size.

Bias-Strip Size

Bias strips are cut in the same fashion as regular bias squares. Add ¼" to the cut size of the bias square and cut strips that width.

Making Side-by-Sides

Using the dimensions just mentioned and the standard techniques for bias-square construction given in Section II, pages 45–48, sew bias strata and cut bias squares from them.

For example, if you want to construct presewn side-by-side units that are ½" finished size on the long edge, add ⅞" to this size to determine the size of the bias squares (½" + ⅞" = 1⅜"). The size of the bias strips you will need to form a multiple bias strata for these 1⅜" bias squares is ¼" larger than the bias square (1⅜"+¼"=1⅝").

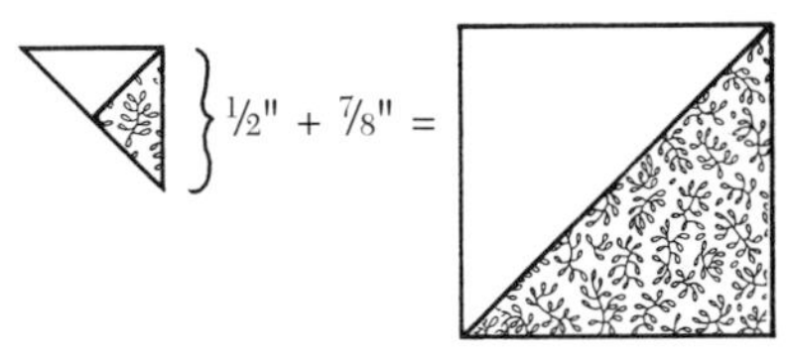

1⅜" bias squares to yield 2 side-by-sides each + ¼" = 1⅝" bias strips

Once the 1⅜" bias squares are cut, turn them on point and cut in half on the diagonal that is not seamed. They are now ready to be used in the block assembly.

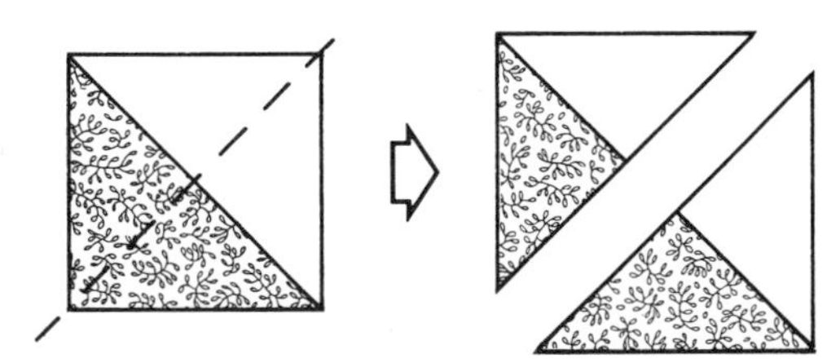

All the patterns in this section require you to use bias strips to construct the bias squares for the side-by-sides because the straight grain is on the long edges. There may be other instances, however, when the long edges should be bias. In that case, seam straight-of-grain strips together and cut the bias squares from these units.

Be sure to work with the warm-up project until you are comfortable with the skills it presents before moving on to the other patterns. Also, remember to check the accuracy of each seam before trimming it to ⅛".

Warm-Up Project: Rolling Star

10¼" x 10¼"

This warm-up project incorporates both side-by-side units and bias squares in its construction. When joining the side-by-side units to form the four-triangle patch, be careful not to stretch the seams, as they are on the bias.

Rolling Star block
Finished size: 2¼"

Cutting Requirements

Fabric #1: Brick print, 9" square
Cut: 1 square, 6" x 6" (side-by-side bias squares)
4 strips, ¾" x 7" (inner border)
4 squares, ¾" x ¾" (inner border corner squares)

Fabric #2: Pale peach print, 14" square
Cut: 2 squares, 6" x 6" (side-by-side bias squares)
1 square, 4¾" x 4¾" (side set triangles)
3 squares, 2¾" x 2¾" (corner triangles and alternate plain block)

Fabric #3: Dark green print, 7" x 13" piece
Cut: 1 square, 6" x 6" (side-by-side bias squares)
1 square, 6" x 6" (regular bias squares)

Fabric #4: Medium green print, 7" x 13" piece
Cut: 1 square, 6" x 6" (regular bias squares)
4 squares, 1¼" x 1¼" (Rolling Star center squares)
4 strips, 2" x 8" (outer border)
4 squares, 2" x 2" (outer border corner squares)

Backing and Binding: 12" square, your fabric choice. To mimic model, use Fabric #4 and a rolled binding (see page 84).

Assembly Instructions

1. Combine the various 6" squares in the following combinations and cut bias strips and squares as indicated. Sew multiple bias strata for maximum production.
   a. Fabric #3 + Fabric #2: Cut 1⅞" strips and 1⅝" bias squares; you will need 8 bias squares. Press to Fabric #3.
   b. Fabric #3 + Fabric #4: Cut 1½" strips and 1¼" bias squares; you will need 16 bias squares. Press to Fabric #4.
   c. Fabric #1 + Fabric #2: Cut 1⅞" strips and 1⅝" bias squares; you will need 8 bias squares. Press to Fabric #1.
2. Cut the 1⅝" bias squares from steps a and c in half on the diagonal to produce 16 side-by-side units from each combination.

3. Join the side-by-sides together as indicated in the diagram to form 16 four-triangle squares. Press the seams away from the Fabric #1/Fabric #2 unit.

4. Lay the Rolling Star units on the work table as in the diagram and seam them into rows. Press seams toward the corner bias squares. Join the rows to form the completed block. Press the seams toward the outer edges.

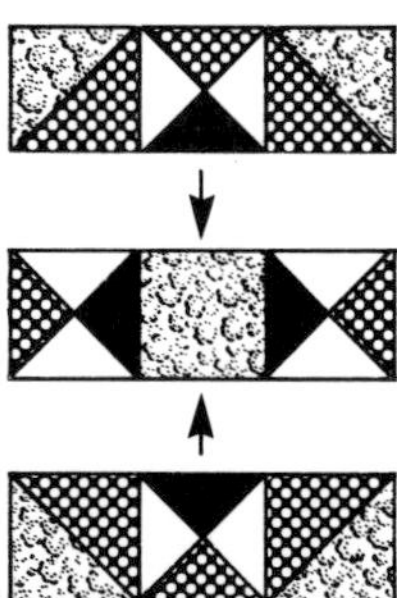

5. Cut the 4¾" Fabric #2 square in half on both diagonals to form 4 quarter-square triangles. These are the quilt's side set triangles. Cut 2 of the 2¾" Fabric #2 squares in half on one diagonal to form 4 half-square triangles. These are the quilt's corner triangles.
6. Lay the plain and pieced blocks, the side triangles, and the corner triangles on the work table as in the diagram. Join them to form the rows as indicated. Press the seams toward the unpieced units. Join the rows to form the quilt top. Press the seams toward the outer edges of the quilt. Add the corner triangles last. Press seams away from the pieced blocks.

7. Cut the 4 Fabric #1 inner border strips to fit the center width of the quilt. Join 2 strips to opposite sides of the quilt. Press the seams toward the strips. Add the inner border corner squares to both ends of the 2 remaining strips. Press the seams toward the strips and seam them to the 2 remaining quilt sides. Press the seams toward the strips.
8. Attach the Fabric #4 outer border strips in the same fashion.
9. Quilt and bind as desired.

Rolling Star *by Donna Lynn Thomas, 1990, Frankfurt, West Germany, 10¼" x 10¼". Peach-colored star points offer a nice contrast to the dark green and brick prints. Quilted by Regine Sauder.*

Scrap Windmill

7" x 8⅜"

This quaint old-time pattern is a great way to use up scraps from previous projects. I used the color-recipe concept in choosing the pieces for this quilt. Rather than randomly choosing scraps, I assigned color families to each position in a block, bringing order to the selection process. In my Windmill block, I chose to assign dark blues to the large triangles, reds to the small inner triangles, and tans to the outer small triangles. I then looked for leftover red-and-tan bias squares that were 1¾" or larger and cut them back to 1⅜". Next, I looked for dark blue triangles or squares that were 1¾" or larger. Don't panic, though, if you don't have a scrap collection of bias squares. You'll find tips on how to achieve a scrap look without a lot of scraps.

Block A **Block B**

Windmill blocks

Finished size: 1"

Cutting Requirements

Fabric #1: Assorted scraps
Cut: 24 red/tan bias squares*, 1⅜" x 1⅜" (side-by-sides)
24 dark blue squares, 1⅜" x 1⅜" (large triangles)

Fabric #2: Tan print, 5" x 15" piece
Cut: 4 strips, ⅞" x 15" (sashings)

Fabric #3: Small red plaid, 9" square
Cut: 4 strips, 1¾" x 9" (outer border)

Backing and Binding: 11" square, your fabric choice. To mimic model, use a navy solid and a rolled binding.

*If you do not have a ready supply of leftover bias squares, cut an assortment of 12 red 2" squares and 12 tan 2" squares. Cut all the squares in half on the diagonal. Randomly sew the red triangles to the tan triangles and cut 1⅜" bias squares from the combinations.

Assembly Instructions

1. Cut the 1⅜" red/tan bias squares in half on the diagonal to form 48 side-by-side triangle units. Cut the 1⅜" blue squares in half on the diagonal to form 48 large triangles.
2. Sew each side-by-side to a large triangle and press the seams toward the large triangles. Square the blocks to 1", if necessary. You should have two types of squares as shown in the diagram. Separate them into two piles.

Squares for Block A

Squares for Block B

3. Make 6 Windmill blocks from each of the 2 piles as shown in the diagram, being careful not to intermix the different units. Join 2 squares to form rows. Butt the center diagonal seams of the squares to help make a tight fit. Press the seams toward the large triangles. Join 2 rows to form the completed block. Press seams in either direction.

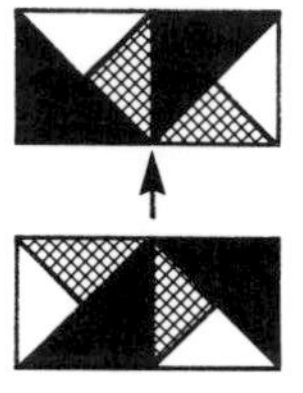

Block A

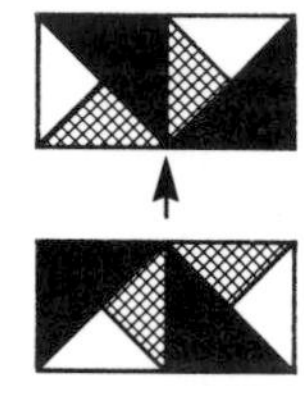

Block B

4. Lay the blocks in a pleasing arrangement 3 across and 4 down. Your Windmill blocks should now be 1½" square. Cut eight 1½" sashing strips from the ⅞" Fabric #2 strips. Attach the ⅞" x 1½" short sashings to the right sides of the blocks in the first and second columns. Press toward the sashings.
5. Join the blocks in horizontal rows. Press seams toward the sashings.
6. Measure the width of each row. They should be 4⅜" wide. Cut 3 sashings the width of the rows from the ⅞" Fabric #2 strips. Sew these center sashings to the bottom of the 3 horizontal rows and make extension marks on the raw edges, indicating the location of the interior short sashing seams. Press seams toward the sashings.

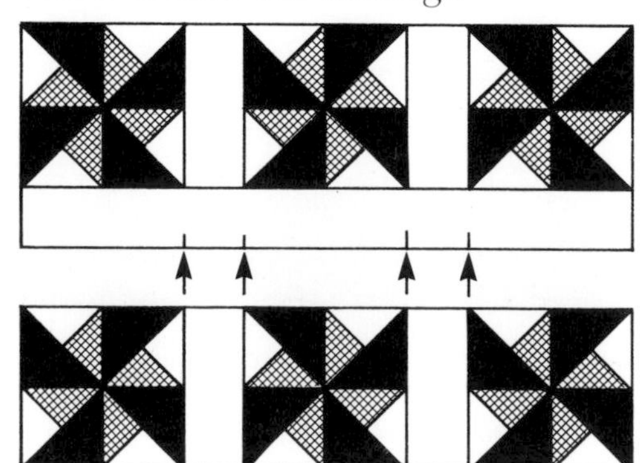

Use extension marks on wrong side to match short sashings

7. Aligning the guide marks with the short sashes of the next row, join the rows together. Press seams toward the sashings.
8. Cut the side sashing strips to fit the length of the quilt through the center. Sew them to either side. Press seams toward the sashings.
9. Measure the top and bottom sashings to fit the width of the quilt through the center and sew them on. Again, press the seams toward the sashings.
10. Following the directions for straight-set borders on page 23, attach the Fabric #3 outer border strips.
11. Quilt and bind as desired.

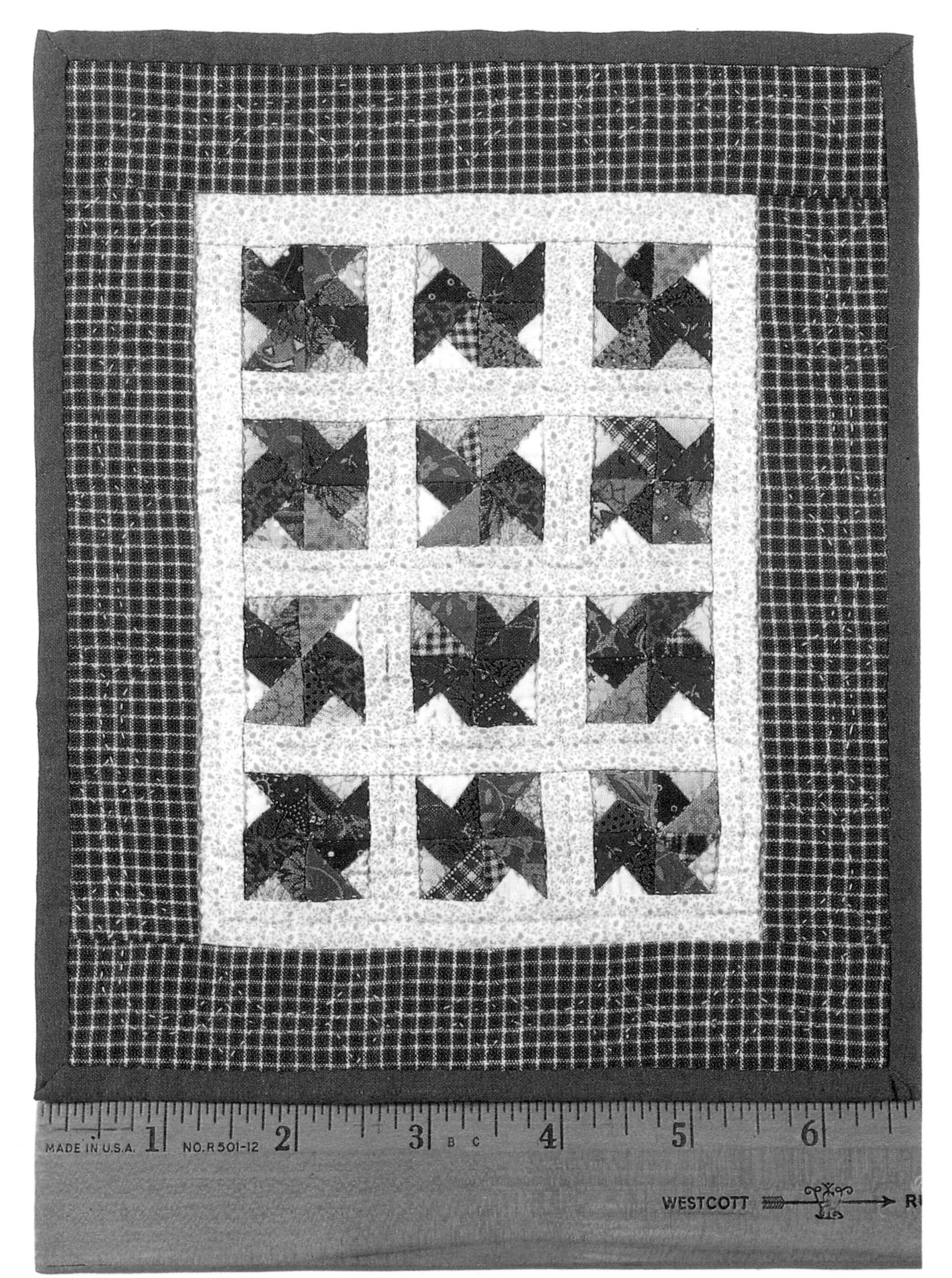

***Scrap Windmill** by Donna Lynn Thomas, 1990, Frankfurt, West Germany, 7" x 8⅜". Dark blue, red, and tan combine to make a striking Windmill block. The tiny red, white, and black plaid is the perfect finish for this charming little quilt.*

Posie Pot

7½" x 9"

This little quilt came about because I absolutely had to use a newly bought striped fabric. After playing with a number of design ideas, I came up with the idea of a striped flowerpot. Even so, it is not necessary for you to use a striped fabric for the pot—a checked or mottled porcelain-like print would work equally well. Here's a chance to be creative.

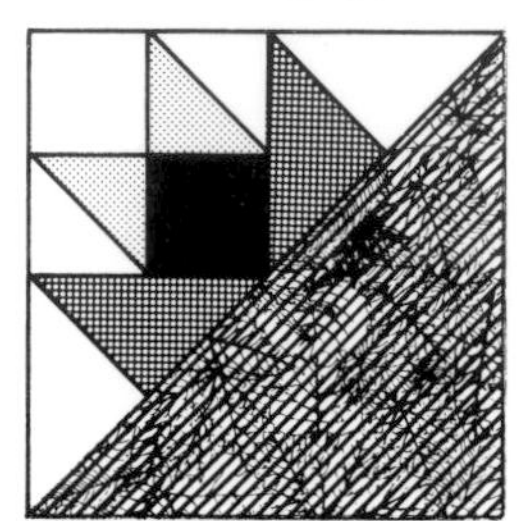

Posie Pot block
Finished size: 1½"

Cutting Requirements

Fabric #1: Green solid, 8" square
Cut: 1 square, 8" x 8" (side-by-side bias squares)

Fabric #2: Red solid, 6" x 9" piece
Cut: 12 squares, ⅞" x ⅞" (posie block centers)
4 strips, ¾" x 9" (outer border)

Fabric #3: Medium rose solid, 6" square
Cut: 1 square, 6" x 6" (regular bias squares—posie points)

Fabric #4: Light teal print, 14" x 15" piece
Cut: 1 square, 8" x 8" (side-by-side bias squares)
1 square, 6" x 6" (regular bias squares—posie points)
12 squares, ⅞" x ⅞" (posie block corners)
4 strips, 1½" x 8" (inner border)

Fabric #5: Striped fabric or border print, approximately ¼ yd. (may be less)
Cut: 2½" wide strips of the portion(s) you wish to use. Cut the strips parallel to the selvage or in the direction of the stripe. Using the Bias Square®, cut six 2⅜" squares from the strips and then cut the squares in half on the diagonal to yield 12 triangles for the flowerpots.

Use the Bias Square® to cut 2⅜" squares from the striped fabric. Cut the squares in half to form large half-square triangles.

Backing: 8" x 10" piece, your fabric choice
Binding: To mimic applied binding on model, use 1 Fabric #5 strip, 1¼" x 42", cut selvage to selvage.

Assembly Instructions

1. Steam the 8" Fabric #1 and Fabric #4 squares right sides together. Cut 1⅞" bias strips from them and sew a multiple bias strata. Press the seams toward Fabric #4. Cut 1⅝" bias squares from the strata; you will need 12. Cut these bias squares in half on the diagonal to form 24 side-by-side units.

2. Steam the 6" Fabric #3 and Fabric #4 squares right sides together and cut 1⅛" bias strips. Seam them into a multiple bias strata, press seams toward Fabric #3, and cut ⅞" bias squares from the strata; you will need 24.
3. Lay the bias squares, ⅞" Fabric #2 squares, and ⅞" Fabric #4 squares on the work table as in the diagram. Assemble the plain squares and the bias squares into Four-Patch units as indicated. Press the seams toward the plain squares.

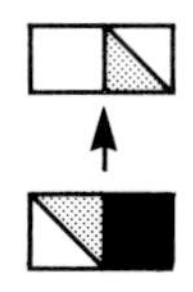

4. Join a side-by-side unit to either side of the Four-Patch unit. Be careful to sew the correct side-by-side to each side. Press the seams toward the side-by-side units.

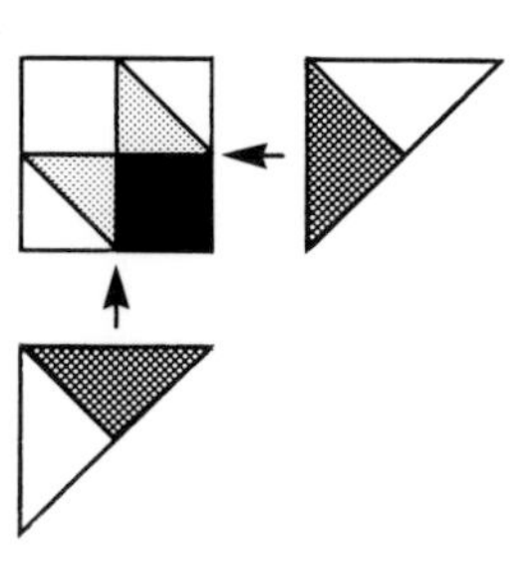

5. Sew a large striped triangle to the long edge of each posie triangle to complete the block. Press the seams toward the striped triangle.

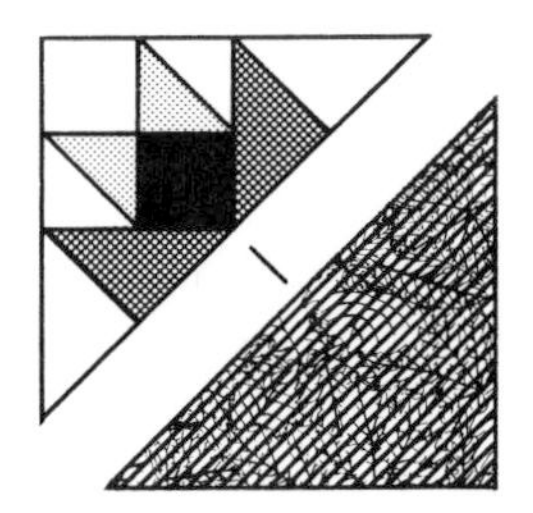

6. Seam the blocks together to form 4 rows of 3 blocks each. Press the seams in each row in one direction but press each row in the opposite direction of the row above it so they butt against each other when joining.
7. Join the rows to form the quilt center. Press the seams in any direction.
8. Following the directions for straight-set borders on page 23, attach the Fabric #4 inner border strips.
9. Attach the Fabric #2 outer border strips in the same fashion.
10. Quilt as desired. See pages 84–86, for instructions on attaching an applied binding.

Posie Pot *by Donna Lynn Thomas, 1989, Broomall, Pennsylvania, 7½" x 9". A striped print for the "pots" is repeated in the border, creating a lively quilt.*

Ohio Star

7⅜" x 7⅜"

The Ohio Star is one of my favorite traditional blocks. I couldn't resist making one in miniature. Since the side-by-sides finish up to be very tiny, it is important to choose fabric prints that do not disappear where they meet other prints at the seams. Remember to keep the contrast high and avoid busy multicolored prints in these areas. A pretty multicolored print would be lovely in the large border, though, to tie the quilt together.

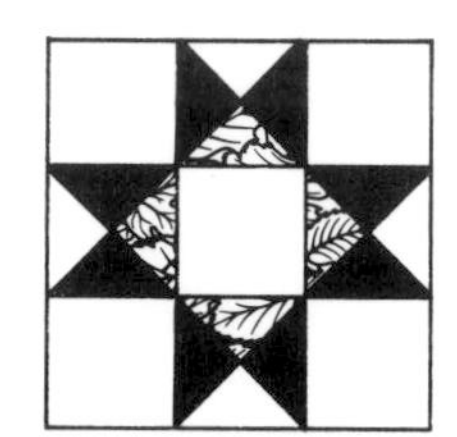

Ohio Star block
Finished size: 1⅛"

Cutting Requirements

Fabric #1: Dark teal print, 11" x 15" piece
Cut: 2 squares, 7" x 7" (side-by-side bias squares)
4 strips, ¾" x 5½" (inner border)

Fabric #2: Medium mauve solid, 8" square
Cut: 1 square, 7" x 7" (side-by-side bias squares)

Fabric #3: Muslin, 9" x 14" piece
Cut: 1 square, 7" x 7" (side-by-side bias squares)
45 squares, ⅞" x ⅞" (Ohio Star plain squares)

Fabric #4: Medium teal print, 6" x 11" piece
Cut: 6 segments, ¾" x 1⅝" (short inner sashes)
2 strips, ¾" x 4⅜" (wide inner sashes)
4 strips, ¾" x 5¼" (outer sashes)

Fabric #5: Medium mauve print, 7" x 9" piece
Cut: 4 strips, 1½" x 7½" (outer border)

Backing and Binding: 9" square, your fabric choice. To mimic model, use Fabric #5 and a rolled binding.

Assembly Instructions

1. Steam each 7" Fabric #1 square right sides together with the 7" Fabric #2 and Fabric #3 squares. Cut 1½" bias strips from each combination. Seam each combination into a multiple strata and press the seams toward Fabric #1. Cut 1¼" bias squares from each multiple strata; you will need 18. Cut the bias squares in half on the diagonal to form 36 side-by-side units from each fabric pair.
2. Sort the side-by-sides into 2 piles and join them together as indicated in the diagram to form 36 Ohio Star units. Press seams toward the Fabric#1/ Fabric #3 side-by-side units.

3. Lay the ⅞" Fabric #3 squares on the work table along with the Ohio Star units. Join them to form horizontal rows and press the seams toward the plain squares. Join the rows to form the Ohio Star blocks. Press the seams toward the outside edges.

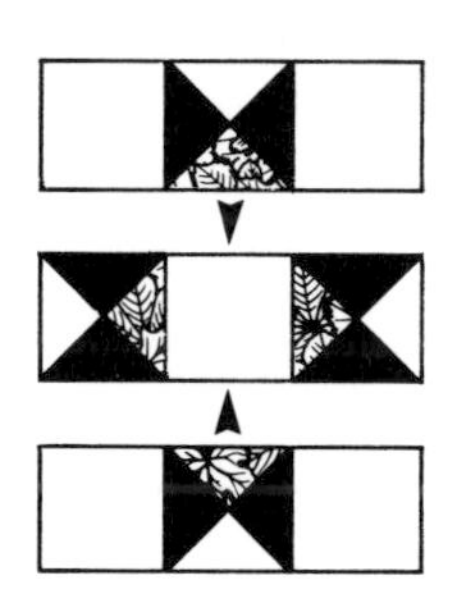

4. Lay the blocks 3 across and 3 down. Sew a ¾" x 1⅝" short sashing to the right side of the first 2 blocks in each horizontal row. Press the seams toward the sashings.
5. Join the 3 blocks in each row together and press the seams toward the sashings.
6. Add a ¾" x 4⅜" Fabric #4 sashing to the bottom of the top 2 rows and press the seams toward the sashings. On the wrong side, make marks on the raw edge of the bottom sashings to indicate the location of the interior short sashing seams.

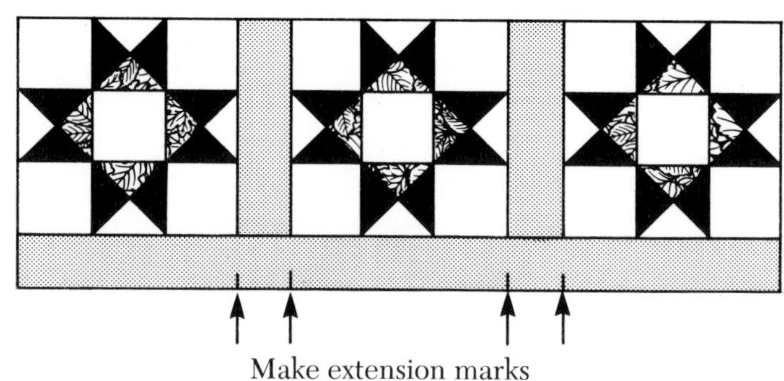

Make extension marks
to indicate short sashing seams

7. Using the marks as guides for aligning the short sashes, join the rows together. Press the seams toward the sashes.
8. Cut 2 of the ¾" x 5¼" Fabric #4 sashes to fit the length of the quilt through the center. Seam them to the sides. Press seams toward outside edges.
9. Cut the remaining 2 sashes to fit the width of the quilt through the center. Seam them to the top and bottom and press seams toward outside edges.
10. Following the directions for straight-set borders on page 23, attach the Fabric #1 inner border strips.
11. Attach the wide Fabric #5 outer border strips in the same fashion.
12. Quilt and bind as desired.

***Ohio Star** by Donna Lynn Thomas, 1990, Frankfurt, West Germany, 7⅜" x 7⅜". The lively teals and mauves in this miniature quilt cause the traditional Ohio Star to twinkle.*

Finishing Up

Generally speaking, the methods for quilting and binding miniature quilts are the same as for full-size quilts, with a few exceptions. This section will show you how to mark quilting designs and how to layer and baste the quilt sandwich. Also included are tips on quilting and two methods of binding the edges.

PREPARING THE QUILT SANDWICH

Choosing Quilting Designs

Quilting serves several purposes, the most important being to hold the three layers of the quilt together. Therefore, it is important to do an adequate amount of quilting to serve this purpose. The density of the quilting should be consistent so that one area of the quilt does not pucker or bulge as a result of too little or too much quilting. Keep this in mind when choosing your designs—a heavily quilted border will also require heavy quilting in the interior of the quilt. If this is not possible, you will need to adjust the border design to accommodate what you are able to do throughout the rest of the quilt. Remember that large areas should not be left unquilted when using a cotton batt. Try to quilt at least every ½", or closer when possible.

If you examine the quilts in this book, you will notice a lot of quilting-in-the-ditch on the pieced areas, particularly on the smaller blocks. This is because the patchwork is so tiny that decorative quilting is pretty much out of the question. When I felt that the visibility of the stitching itself would detract from the patchwork, I chose a quilting thread to match the fabrics. Other times, I felt the stitching would enhance the design and purposely chose thread colors that would show. These are personal decisions you must make for yourself.

In addition to being functional, quilting serves as a means of creative expression. The designs you choose should enhance the quilt pattern. Borders, plain blocks, side set triangles, and open areas provide the opportunity to do some decorative quilting. There are a growing number of commercial miniature quilting stencils and books on the market. They are wonderful additions to your miniature supplies. And don't feel shy about being innovative in your search for home-grown miniature designs. Much can be done with straight or diagonal lines and simple curves derived from coins and other small basic shapes. Echoing a curved shape or following the directional flow of an overall patchwork design are time-honored methods of quilting. Heart and flower designs can be found in many places, such as greeting cards and children's coloring books. Look at the world around you with a quilter's eye.

You'll find a few quilting designs on pages 86–87.

Marking Quilting Designs

Many quilting designs must be marked directly on the quilt top to act as an accurate guide for your quilting stitches. I know there are many quilters who prefer to use lead pencils to mark their quilting designs. With proficiency, these marks are barely noticeable on a full-size quilt. Miniature quilts, by their very nature, beg for close inspection, and pencil marks can seriously detract from their charm. I strongly encourage you to sample the large assortment of high-quality washable markers available at quilt shops and through mail-order quilt supply catalogs. Always be sure to test a new marker on scrap fabric before using it on your quilts.

Give your quilt top a final pressing before marking it. This is also the time to square the edges of the quilt and trim them so they are straight and true.

When marking the designs, work on a hard, flat surface and keep your marking pencils sharp. Other than stencils, the easiest way to transfer designs to a miniature quilt is the use of a light box. Even a light box is not necessary if the day is sunny. Trace the design onto a piece of tissue paper with a black marker. Tape the tissue paper to a bright, sunny window and tape the quilt top over the design (try engineer's masking tape or artist's white tape as they have less glue). It's easy to see and trace the design onto the quilt when the sun is shining through the tissue paper and fabric.

Preparing the Batting and Backing

Because the batting needs to be peeled in half to create a loft consistent with the size of the quilt, I use a 100% cotton batt. I have found the new cotton batts very easy to peel.

Peel the cotton batt in half

The choice of a backing depends on which type of binding you intend to use. A rolled binding is a binding created by rolling the backing to the front. It is frequently used in miniatures and means that the choice of a backing must coordinate with the front.

An applied binding is cut and applied independently of the back. Therefore, the backing can be any print or solid you choose, whether it coordinates or not. Just as with the front, use tightly woven, good-quality cotton.

Layer top on batting and backing

Both batting and backing should be cut an inch or two larger than the quilt top on all four sides to allow for the 5% loss in quilt dimension when the layers are quilted. Press the backing smooth after cutting it and smooth the batting flat and wrinkle free.

Layering and Basting

After the quilting designs are marked and the batting and backing prepared, you are ready to secure the quilt sandwich (backing, batting, and quilt top) with basting stitches. Press the backing smooth and tape it right side down to a hard, flat work surface (a rotary mat works beautifully). Securely tape the sides of the backing every few inches. Tape the corners last, being careful not to stretch the bias. Lay the peeled batting with the interior side of it face up. Smooth it and center the pressed and marked quilt top on top of the batting right side up. Beginning in the center and working out toward the edges, pin the three layers together so that they are smooth and flat. Baste the sandwich with a light-colored thread from the center out, in a 1"–1½" grid.

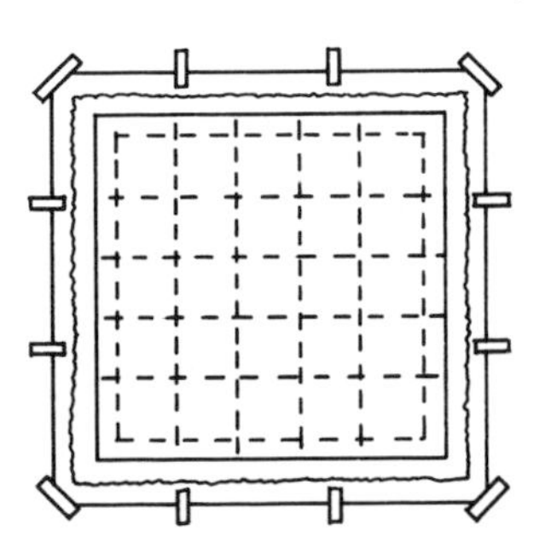

Finish by basting a line of stitches around the edge of the quilt. Remove the pins.

QUILTING AND BINDING

Quilting is a simple running stitch that goes through all three layers of the quilt sandwich. Just as with large quilts, all quilting should be done from the center out.

With miniatures, I do not limit myself to quilting threads. The threads you use should be fine, not thick, 100% cotton threads or, as a second choice, cotton-covered polyester. A fine quilting thread in the color you desire is ideal. If you cannot find the right weight and color of quilting thread, do not hesitate to search through your regular sewing threads for the right color.

Since the size of these quilts is small, reduce your thread length accordingly. You will want to use the smallest needle you can comfortably handle, and the eye on a size 10 or 12 needle will wear out the thread as it runs back and forth through it. Therefore, if the thread is short, about 10"–12", it will be in the needle for only a short time and will not become worn or tangled the way a longer thread would.

Most quilters prefer to use a quilting frame of some shape or size when quilting. The natural inclination would be to scale down to a small embroidery hoop when working on a miniature. However, a peeled batting is likely to tear with the stress of the tight tension created by a hoop. It is much easier to fold the excess quilt in your nonquilting hand while quilting. You may find yourself almost weaving the quilt up and down onto the needle as you become more comfortable with the technique. By all means, continue to use whatever thimbles you prefer.

Begin quilting with a small single knot, which is tied close to the end of the thread. Slip the needle between the layers of the quilt about a needle length's distance from your chosen starting point. If possible, weave the needle through a seam allowance. Bring the needle up where you want to start and give the thread a tug to lodge the knot in the batting.

Following the quilting marks, sew a simple running stitch, being sure to catch all three layers with each stitch. Ideally, the stitches on the back of the quilt should be the same size as the stitches on the front. All stitches should be of consistent size and evenly spaced. It is better to sacrifice small stitch size in favor of even spacing and consistent size. End a line of quilting by forming a small knot in the thread about ⅛" from where it exits the quilt. Take the last stitch between the layers only and run the needle a distance away from the last stitch before bringing the needle up, out of the quilt. Again, weaving the thread in and out of a seam allowance before exiting will strengthen the quilting. A gentle tug and the knot will slip between the layers. Clip the thread a short distance from the quilt top and let the tail slip back between the layers.

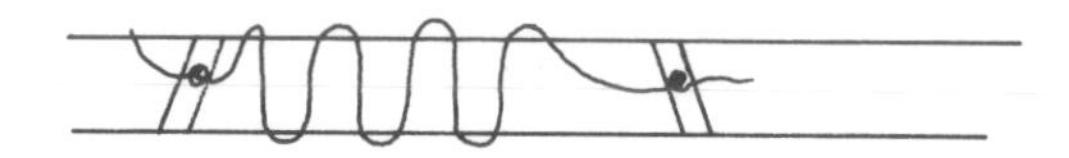

Weaving the thread in and out of the seam allowance strengthens the quilting

Sometimes, you may have to cross an intersection that has bulky seams. In such a situation, take one stitch at a time, using a technique known as stab-stick.

Push the needle through the quilt where the next stitch should be. Before pulling the needle through, turn the quilt over and make sure the needle is in its proper position on the back. Adjust, if necessary, and pull the needle to the back. Reverse the process to return the needle to the top.

Continue in this manner until you pass the bulky intersection. This may seem tedious but it eliminates big gaps in the line of quilting. Continue to quilt, working from the center of the quilt toward the edges to ease out any fullness. If you work from the edges in, you may lock any fullness in the center of the quilt. Finish all the quilting and remove the basting stitches before binding the quilt.

Rolled Binding

A rolled binding is a simple finish to a miniature quilt. Be sure to choose a backing fabric that is suitable for the finished edge of your quilt because the backing is rolled to the front in a rolled binding. Avoid one-way or directional prints. To use these types of prints, you need to make an applied binding.

Once you have completed the quilting, fold the backing out of the way under the quilt and trim the batting even with the quilt top. True up the quilt-top edges, if necessary. Next, cut the backing to exactly ½" from the quilt top. Make sure the corners are square. Fold the backing in half on one side so that its raw edge butts against the quilt top. Roll the folded backing to the front of the quilt and secure it in place with pins.

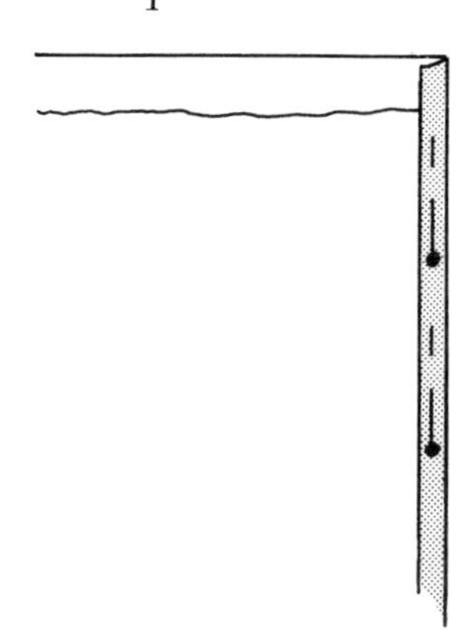

Fold the backing in half and roll the fold to the front edge of the quilt. Pin in place.

At the corner, fold the rolled backing in as in the diagram. The outer edge of the fold should now be butted against the adjacent quilt-top edge. The corner fold should be at a 45° angle to the sides.

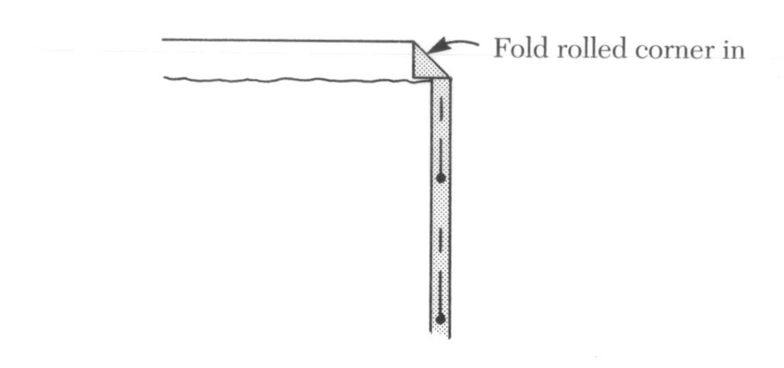

Now, working on the next side, continue to fold under the raw edge of the backing and roll to the front, securing it with pins. Turn the corner into a neat miter and pin in place.

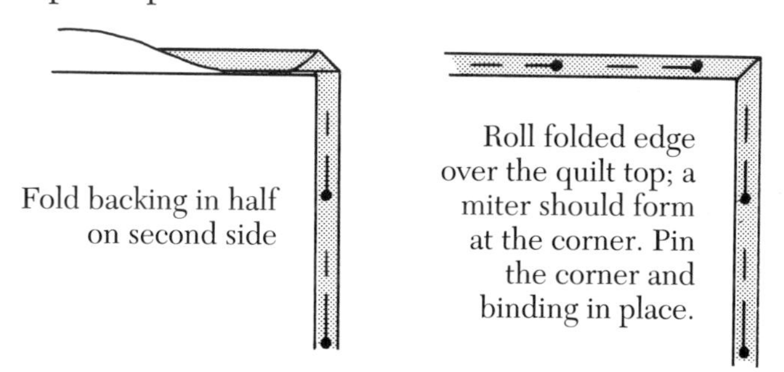

Fold backing in half on second side

Roll folded edge over the quilt top; a miter should form at the corner. Pin the corner and binding in place.

After the backing is completely pinned, slip-stitch it closed with matching thread. Be sure to stitch the corner miters closed.

Applied Binding

An applied binding gives you some creative options that you do not have with a rolled binding. Stripes make an interesting finish, and bindings can even be pieced if you are feeling adventuresome. Look at the photo of Posie Pot on page 79 for an example of a striped binding. Instructions in the Posie Pot pattern on how to cut the binding can be applied to any pattern of your choosing.

Determine the amount of binding needed by adding the measurements of all four sides plus about 6"–8" for corners and joining the ends. Selvage-to-selvage strips are good because you normally need only one or two strips.

When joining two binding strips, seam them together with a diagonal seam to evenly disperse the seam allowance. To do this, lay the two strips right sides together at right angles to each other; pin. Seam them from corner to corner on the outer corners as in the diagram. Cut away the excess and press the seam in either direction.

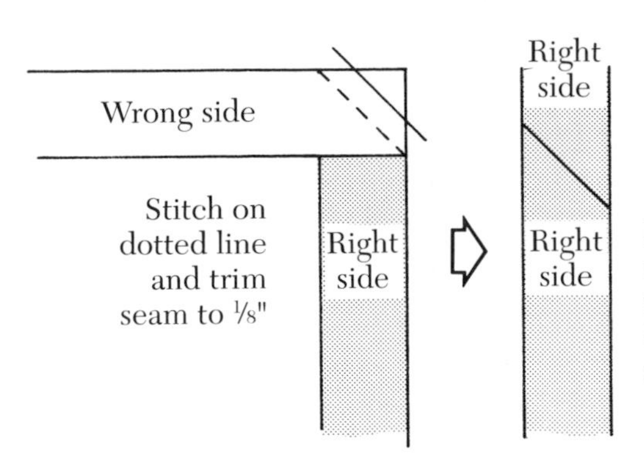

Cut the batting and backing even with the quilt top. True up the edges and corners, if necessary. Baste the three layers of the quilt securely at the outer edges if you already have removed the previous basting.

Lay the binding strip right sides together on the front edge of the quilt, with the tail about one third in from the left corner.

Place a pin ¼" in from the right-hand corner. Leaving about 4"–6" of the tail free, stitch the binding to the quilt with a ¼" seam allowance. Stop at the ¼" mark, backstitch, and remove quilt from the machine.

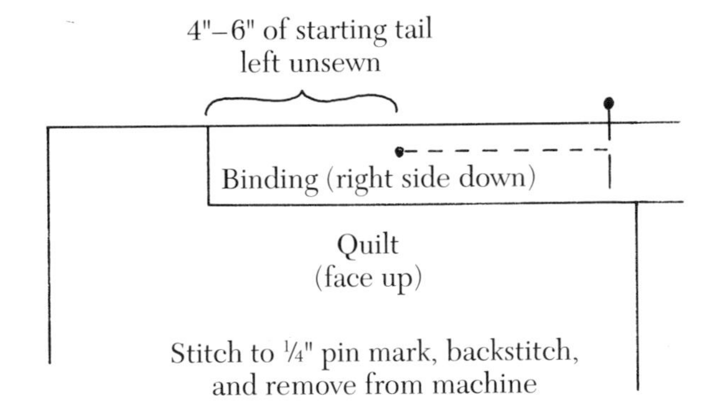

Flip the binding straight up from the corner so that it forms a continuous line with the adjacent side.

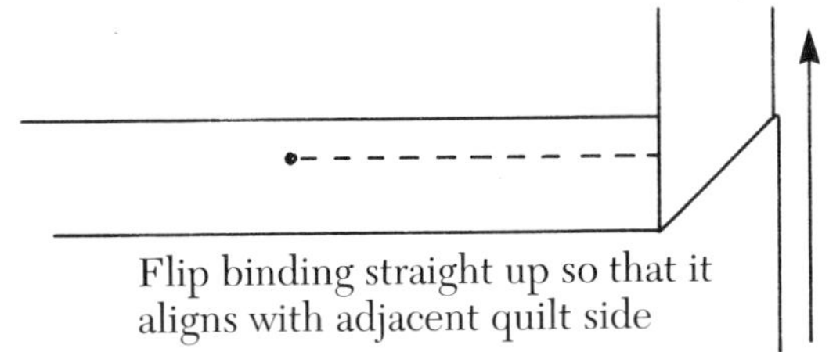

Now, fold the binding straight down so that it lays on top of the adjacent side, being careful not to shift the pleat formed at the fold.

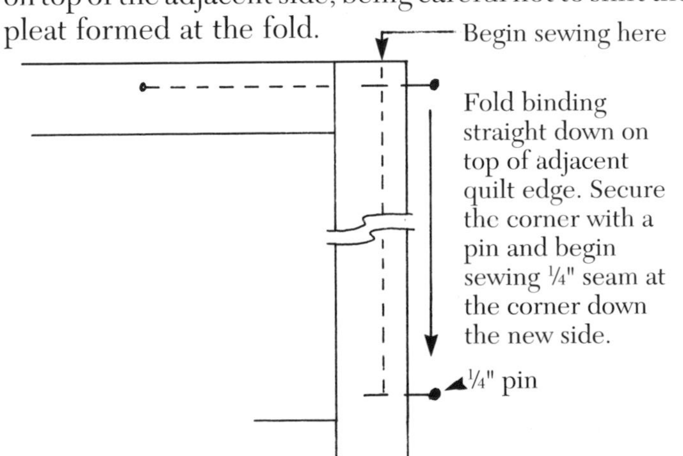

Pin the pleat in place and again mark the next corner with a pin ¼" from the edge. Stitch this new side with a ¼" seam just to the pin and repeat the process for turning the corner as before.

After turning the fourth corner, stitch only about 1" of the fourth side. You should be back to the side where you started. Cut excess off remaining tail of binding so that only about 3"–4" overlaps the starting tail.

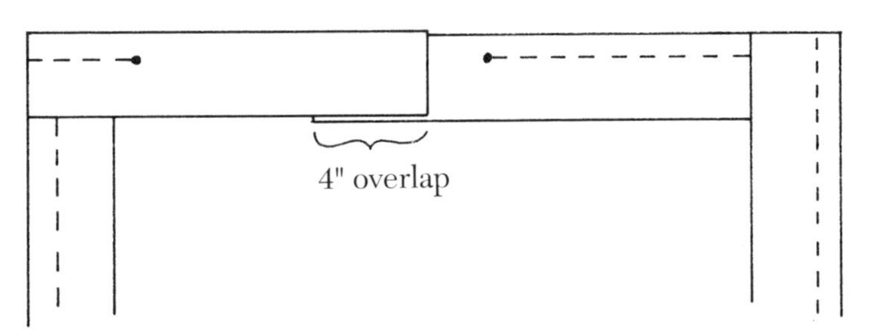

Fold the ending tail out of the way and cut the starting tail with a 45° diagonal cut. If you have a 45° line on your ruler, use that to make the cut. If you do not have such a marking, measure in from the end of the tail on the wrong side a distance equal to the width of the starting tail and draw a pencil line to form a square. Cut the square on the diagonal.

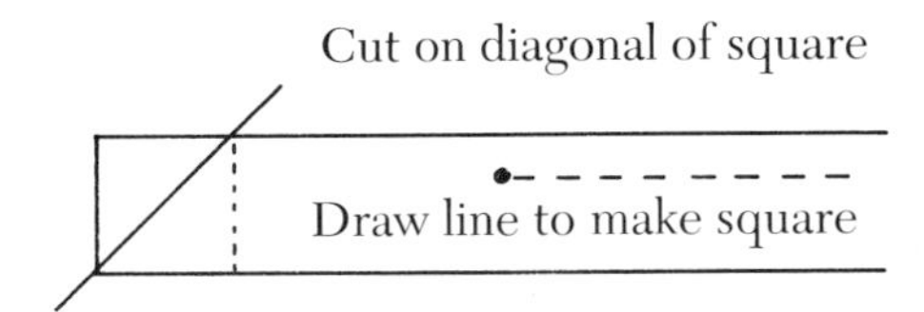

The ending tail now needs to be cut to match the starting tail. Lay the ending tail under the starting tail and draw a diagonal line to match the diagonal cut of the starting tail. Cut the ending tail ½" longer than this line.

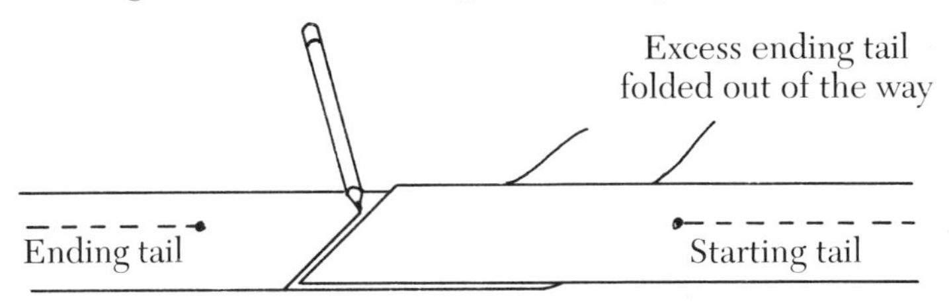

Draw line on ending tail to match diagonal cut of starting tail

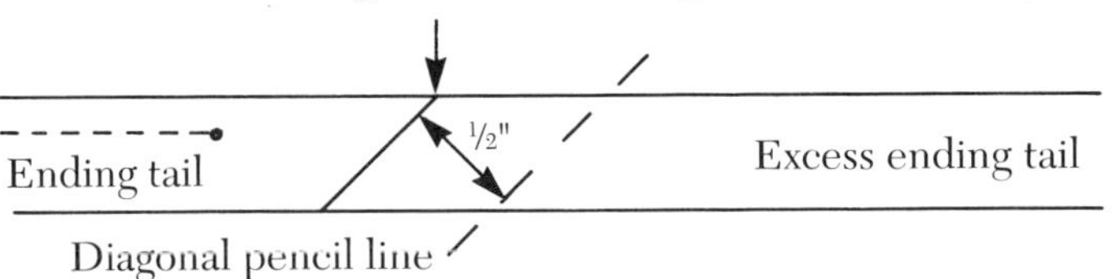

Cut tail ½" longer than diagonal pencil line

Join the tails right sides together, offsetting them by 1/4" so that they align after sewing; press. The tails should now be joined so that they fit the remaining distance exactly.

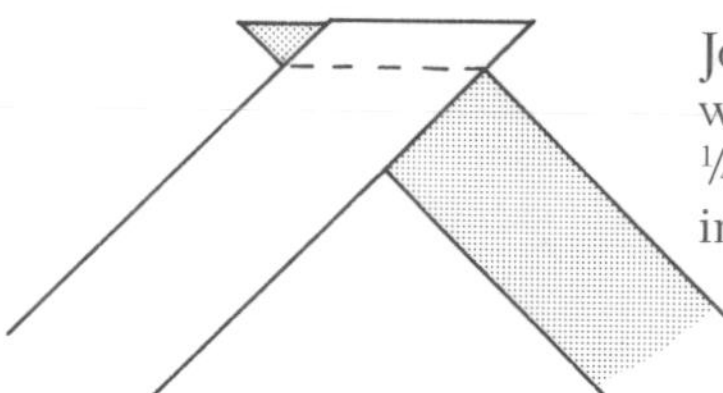

Join tails right sides together with 1/4" seam. Offset corners so 1/4" seam starts and stops at intersection.

Finish sewing the binding in place and turn it to the back of the quilt. Turn the raw edge under 1/4" and slip-stitch it in place with a matching thread. Miter the corners on the back as you come to them (the fabric will fold and turn almost automatically into a miter). Slip-stitch the miters closed. Your quilt is now ready to be signed and dated.

CARE OF MINIATURES

Since miniatures are easily washed in a sink or small tub, they are easy to care for. Use the same soaps as discussed on page 9.

When the quilt is finished, wash it to remove the chalk markings. Generally, this should be one of the very few washings your miniature should ever need. Since it will not be used in a functional manner, it will probably not soil. Dust can be brushed or gently shaken off, while true soiling or stains will require laundering.

Because the cotton batting has been split, the washing should be very gentle. Generally, all that is needed is a soaking in soapy water, followed by a rinsing in clear water. Let the water drain from the sink and press the remaining water from the quilt. Do not wring or twist the quilt in any way. Lay the quilt on a nice plump towel, reshape, if necessary, and let dry. When the top feels dry, turn the quilt over and put it on another dry towel until the back is completely dry.

With proper care, your miniature treasure should charm and enchant others for generations. For their sake, please attach a muslin label to the back of your quilt with your name, date, and location. If there's a story to go with the quilt, jot it down and attach it to the quilt, or keep it with the quilt when you store it.

Quilting Designs

Bibliography

Hargrave, Harriet. *Heirloom Machine Quilting*. Westminster, California: Burdett Publications, 1987.

Hickey, Mary. *Little By Little: Quilts in Miniature*. Bothell, Washington: That Patchwork Place, Inc., 1988.

Hughes, Trudie. *Template-Free™ Quiltmaking*. Bothell, Washington: That Patchwork Place, Inc., 1986.

Hughes, Trudie. *More Template-Free™ Quiltmaking*. Bothell, Washington: That Patchwork Place, Inc., 1987.

Hughes, Trudie. *Even More*. Bothell, Washington: That Patchwork Place, Inc., 1989.

Malone, Maggie. *1001 Patchwork Designs*. New York: Sterling Publishing Company, Inc., 1982.

Marston, Gwen, and Cunningham, Joe. *American Beauties: Rose and Tulip Quilts*. Paducah, Kentucky: American Quilter's Society, 1988.

Martin, Nancy J. *Pieces of the Past*. Bothell, Washington: That Patchwork Place, Inc., 1986.

Martin, Nancy J. *Back to Square One*. Bothell, Washington: That Patchwork Place, Inc., 1988.

McCloskey, Marsha, and Martin, Nancy J. *A Dozen Variables*. Bothell, Washington: That Patchwork Place, Inc., 1987.

McClun, Diana, and Nownes, Laura. *Quilts, Quilts, Quilts: The Complete Guide to Quiltmaking*. San Francisco: Quilt Digest Press, 1988.

Schaefer, Becky. *Working in Miniature*. Lafayette, California: C & T Publishing, 1987.

Twelker, Nancyann Johanson. *Women and Their Quilts*. Bothell, Washington: That Patchwork Place, Inc., 1988.

THAT PATCHWORK PLACE PUBLICATIONS